the
Handwriting
analyst's toolkit

the
handwriting
analyst's toolkit

character and personality revealed through graphology

Peter West

BARRON'S

A QUARTO BOOK

First edition for North America
published in 2004 by
Barron's Educational Series, Inc.

All inquiries should be addressed to:
Barron's Educational Series, Inc.
250 Wireless Boulevard
Hauppauge, NY 11788
http://www.barronseduc.com

International Standard Book Number
0-7641-2792-6

Library of Congress Catalog Card Number
2003110646

QUAR.HTB

Conceived, designed, and produced by
Quarto Publishing plc
The Old Brewery
6 Blundell Street
London N7 9BH

PROJECT EDITOR Jo Fisher
ART EDITOR Sheila Volpe
DESIGNER Tanya Devonshire-Jones
ASSISTANT ART DIRECTOR Penny Cobb
COPY EDITOR Amy Corzine
PROOFREADER Louise Armstrong
PHOTOGRAPHER Les Weis
INDEXER Diana LeCore

ART DIRECTOR Moira Clinch
PUBLISHER Piers Spence

Manufactured by Universal Graphics,
Singapore
Printed by Star Standard Industries,
Singapore

9 8 7 6 5 4 3 2 1

INTRODUCTION **6**

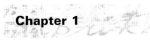

Chapter 1

Chapter 2

CONTENTS

Chapter 3

Chapter 4

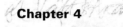

Chapter 5

Introduction

Graphology, or handwriting analysis, is an art science used to interpret character and personality. While handwriting is silent, it is also extremely expressive, reflecting the mood and thoughts of the writer at the time of writing. This accounts for the differences seen in handwriting from day-to-day or even hour-to-hour. It is important to remember that one does not require extrasensory perception to be an analyst and a graphologist cannot foretell future events. However, a skilled analyst should be able to predict the reactions of a writer based on his or her script.

The history of graphology

In 120 A.D., the writer Suetonius gave us perhaps the first ever graphological personality analysis when he criticized the handwriting of the current emperor of the Roman Empire, Octavius Augustus. He noted that the emperor cramped his letters all into one line to avoid starting a new line and suggested that this demonstrated his untrustworthiness.

Kuo Jo-hsu, a Chinese philosopher in the 11th century, alleged that handwriting would reveal whether a letter was written by a noble or a peasant. From then until 1622, references to graphology are rare until Camillo Baldi, a professor at the University of Bologna, published the first known detailed work on handwriting analysis that has since been accepted as the origin of modern graphology.

In the 17th century, the German philosopher Gottfried Leibnitz, commented on the way

At long last graphology really has come of age.

handwriting might reveal character, and in 1792 J. Grohman of Wittenburg wrote a treatise on handwriting. Later, Goethe wrote of his belief in its potential. The word "graphology" itself was not coined until 1871 by a Frenchman, Abbé Jean-Hippolyte Michon, one of the founding fathers of modern handwriting analysis. From the early 18th to the early part of the last century, a growing number of well known and prominent people professed their interest and even ability to read character and personality through handwriting.

The last part of the 20th century saw tremendous advances in techniques of handwriting analysis in North America and Europe. The advent of the Internet has further expanded the potential for development; in these early days of the 21st century, many web-based forums have been created in which graphologists from all over the world discuss old and new material and techniques, thus honing analysis to a level of extreme accuracy.

Getting started

Remember, always take careful note, not of what is written, but of how it has been written. The ideal handwriting sample for any analysis should be around one hundred words long, written on a sheet of unlined paper, and should bear the writer's signature. A normal pen should be used, not a fiber tip and never a pencil. It is preferable to have the sample in prose form and it should not be a copy of anything; a recent letter or notes written over a short period of time is best. Anything written specifically for the purpose of analysis will be too artificial.

Note the pen, the ink color, and the paper quality as these will also help in the final analysis.

Always check to see if the writer is left-handed.

Most graphologists will begin an analysis at the end of the letter and then work back to the beginning. This is because we tend to pay far more attention to our writing style when we begin to write. However, by the time we get to the end of our message, we have often put to one side the formalities of composition and tend to write far more naturally. Each trait revealed in handwriting is only one clue among many and must never be regarded in isolation. The occasional sign is just that—one pointer toward one characteristic. All clues, signs, and traits have both negative and positive aspects to be taken into account. Only when you are satisfied that you have examined every possible feature, should you make your analysis known.

TIP Note what language your sample has been written in. Just because you don't understand the content, it doesn't mean that you can't still read the character of the writer. German handwriting is rather angular when compared to the English or Spanish national style, so it is important to know how relaxed the writer is with the language being written. A native Italian writing in French may have to translate the matter first before putting pen to paper.

How to look for clues

In this exercise we will examine a handwritten letter. There are many different approaches to handwriting analysis, and all practitioners vary in their approach. If there is something in the letter that immediately catches your eye, this should be examined first, and the order suggested here need not be strictly adhered to. After a while you will adopt an approach to suit your personal style.

1 Graphologists are not mind-readers—get as many facts to begin with as you can. What is the age, sex, and education of the writer? Are they left- or right-handed? The language used—is it native to the writer? If not, which style are they more used to? National "hands" can differ quite considerably.

2 Always hold the sample in your hand to feel for the indentations made by the pen, indicating the amount of pressure applied as the words were written (▶▶ *Pressure*, *page 16*).

3 Look at the last couple of lines first and compare them with the first two or three. There will be some differences—the first few lines are almost always created more self-consciously than the last few, so take this into consideration.

4 How has the letter been signed, and is the handwriting of the signature different from that in the body of the script (▶▶ *Signatures*, *page 70; use your toolkit)?*

5 Does the writing recline, incline, or is it upright (▶▶ *Slant*, *page 12; use your toolkit)?*

6 Do the lines slope up or down—or both (▶▶ *Line slope*, *page 42)?*

7 Note the size of the script and the amount of spacing between letters, words, and lines (▶▶ *Size*, *page 18; Spacing*, *page 20; use your toolkit).*

8 Has the writer created good margins and do these change at all throughout the text (▶▶ *Margins*, *page 26; use your toolkit)?*

9 Observe the way the "i" dots and "t"-bars are made (▶▶ *"i" & "t" marks*, *page 62).*

10 Check the punctuation (▶▶ *Punctuation*, *page 60; use your toolkit).*

11 Use a magnifying glass to examine the small details. Look for hooks and ticks, and other odd letter formations (▶▶ *Lead-in strokes*, *page 56; Final strokes*, *page 58; Graphologist's alphabet*, *page 92; use your toolkit).*

12 Where double letters appear, check them carefully for consistency. This will tell you how controlled the writer was at the time the letter was penned.

13 Examine the loop formations to assess the writer's emotional frame of mind (▶▶ *Loops*, *page 34; use your toolkit).*

14 How fast has the text been written (▶▶ *Speed*, *page 44)?*

15 Can you categorize the handwriting as one of the four scripts outlined on page 46?

16 How have the capital letters been constructed (▶▶ *Capital letters*, *page 54; use your toolkit)?*

17 Last, is the envelope still available? How is it addressed (▶▶ *Envelopes*, *page 52; use your toolkit)?* This is also an important source of numbers (▶▶ *Numbers*, *page 120 use your toolkit).*

Anatomy of a letter

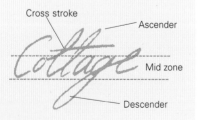

Cross stroke

Ascender

Mid zone

Descender

The graphologist's toolkit

The envelope at the back of the book contains your toolkit which comprises the following essential items:

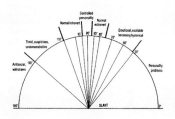

The **protractor** is a key piece of apparatus for measuring the writing angle or slant. The personality characteristics attributed to different angles of writing are clearly displayed. Place the protractor over your sample, lining the base up along the handwriting baseline, to determine the correct angle of your sample (see Slant, page 12).

Lay the **zone gauge** over your sample to delineate the three handwriting zones in order to examine loops, and lead-in and final strokes (see Loops, page 34; Lead-in strokes, page 56; Final strokes, page 58). This grid will also help you to analyze size (page 18), spacing (page 20), and line slope (page 42).

Use the **ruler** to accurately measure size, spacing, and margins (page 26).

Chapter 1

Handwriting Overview

E nter the fascinating world of graphology and learn to uncover the fundamental personality traits hidden in our handwriting. This first chapter discusses the basics of graphology, looking at the features we first notice upon examination of a sample of handwriting, such as slant, size, pressure, and margins. What do variations in these features mean and what can we conclude about a writer's character?

1:1 **Slant**

The way writing is slanted indicates a variety of personality characteristics from introversion to emotional volatility. The toolkit included with this book incorporates a useful protractor to measure slant, which shows the various attributes that are exposed via different angles of writing.

How we learn to write

Long before nursery school, most children have the chance to play with chalk or crayons. Some may graduate to pens or pencils, and experiment with them before starting school. During their first school lessons, however, children are instructed by a teacher who is trained to help them develop alongside their contemporaries.

HOLDING WRITING TOOLS

When people complain that their handwriting is poor, more often than not a simple adjustment to the way they hold their pen is all that is needed. However, making, and then maintaining, any adjustment is not an easy matter, and a lot of patience is necessary.

The best and easiest way to hold a pen is with a soft pincer-like grip between the thumb and the forefinger, with the pen resting against the middle finger. The height of this hold varies from writer to writer, as does the angle of the pen to the paper. The writer's grip should be fairly loose. The more tightly a pen is held, the heavier the pressure a writer tends to apply.

A ballpoint pen should be held slightly more upright than a fountain pen, while a pencil can operate at different levels. Generally speaking, the further along the barrel from the writing tip a pen is held, the better control the writer has over it.

A quick experiment with several different pens will soon illustrate how well you conform to this, but there is no set method to use for greater control of your writing instrument. Whatever you feel the most comfortable with is usually best.

Right-handed pen-hold style

What they are taught first is a print system. The forerunner of cursive handwriting, this is relatively easy to learn.

Children soon develop their own personal style and will modify their handwriting to suit themselves, for few teachers teach a specific style. While children are still quite young, they begin to write at a particular angle to the baseline. Many will adopt one of the three basic slants—that is, a reclined or "backward" slope, an upright style, or an inclined or forward slant.

Whichever style a child initially adopts while learning to write, many exhibit confusion and frustration as they struggle to come to terms with scribbling, drawing, and proper writing. The existing relationship between the hand and the mind has to work overtime to gain ascendancy over the emotional insecurity we all experience at this time.

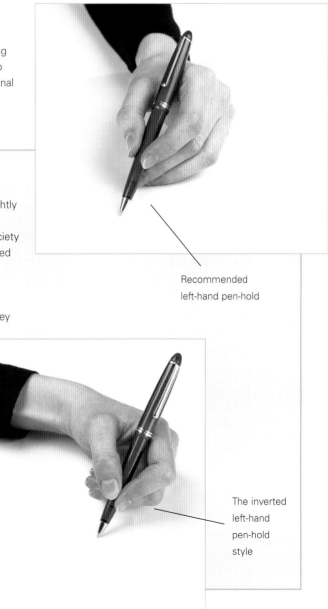

Recommended
left-hand pen-hold

Left-handed style

As a rule, left-handed people of any age will be slightly more perceptive and receptive as they have had to learn to adapt in order to exist successfully in a society geared toward the right-handed. Naturally left-handed children often require extra lessons and good supervision by a perceptive adult to learn how to manage a writing instrument. However, while left-handed youngsters generally learn to write well, they tend to write more slowly than average and often with a "backward" or left slant.

Although the child's body positioning creates this reclined slant, a gently applied adjustment by the teacher will enable him or her to settle into a good writing position.

A left-handed person generally uses a similar pen-holding style to that of a right-handed person. Sometimes an inverted hand position may be adopted, where a hook-style hold is used to pull a pen over a page. Whether a writer is left- or right-handed, there will be variations in the way each individual holds a writing instrument.

The inverted
left-hand
pen-hold
style

In bello parvis momentis magni casus intercedunt

Handwriting slopes to the right

Inclined handwriting When handwriting shows a clearly defined inclination, the writer's decisions tend to be more emotionally based; that is, facts don't always matter to the person. Quite a few writers of this type adopt a "mood of the moment" stance. They tend to be openly compassionate and try to do what others expect of them. However, their occupational interests must be relatively undemanding because, for them, the less effort required the better.

A clearly inclined script implies volcanic emotional responses. These people are "up" one minute and "down" the next. They tend to fall in love with love, and what is exciting at ten in the morning can be forgotten by six in the evening.

A forward-inclining script like this indicates an ardent and responsive nature—that is, someone susceptible to outer influences who is very easily sidetracked. Such people are impulsive, restless, and unsettled; for them, feelings almost always influence their decisions. They are also physically demonstrative with their feelings.

Be free to be who you really are, gorgeous, talented and in love. Becoming healthy, happy and at peace. Sharing in true, loving relationships

Script slopes backward

Reclined handwriting No formal school of handwriting anywhere in the world advocates a backward slope, so this must always be read by a graphologist as a sign of a rebel streak. People who write in this manner are usually awkward and emotionally defensive. More often than not, they have been hurt emotionally and tend to hide their real feelings from others; as a result, they may lack spontaneity in their responses.

People who write like this maintain a calm exterior and appear to be in control but are very different inwardly. They often have a feeling that they are being watched, and it is hard for them to trust anyone. They have few close friends, but a surprising number of acquaintances. Extremely reclined handwriting indicates a highly sensitive, emotional nature and poor adaptability. People with such a handwriting style adopt a regular routine and distrust anyone or anything new to their circle, because it introduces change and uncertainty.

Around puberty, youngsters often adopt a backward slope, which may reflect the rebellious inclinations that children often have at that age. As early romances come to an end, this may be seen more often as they strive to hide their feelings while trying to outwardly maintain ambivalence.

Hope it's okay in this colour ~ This is absolutely my favourite pen (wonder what that says about me!)

Vertical handwriting This script is consistently upright, tending away from the vertical by, at most, four or five degrees on either side. It shows a writer with a head-over-heart attitude to everything and everyone. Such people are always open to suggestion, but are cautious and like to keep control of situations at all times. If this slips for any reason, they will spend a lot of time restoring the status quo.

These people flourish well when they take charge, and especially shine in an emergency. They know how to keep their heads and have a natural air of authority that other people follow as a matter of course. These writers prefer to deal with facts, not fiction. Should such people's writing recline slightly, they will exhibit a little more caution than average. When this kind of script inclines slightly, the writer will be more active and sociable. Such people fall naturally into positions of authority.

Consistently upright script

Left-slanting letter

I am a fifty yr old female, who h to admit it. I have three grown childre and two grandchildren, who are everything. My husband, is a self employed carpenter ...

Right-slanting letter

Unstable or mixed slant For some people, slant can and does vary considerably, even within the same line in a single sample. When you see this, it shows the natural impulses of the writer were unstable at the time of writing.

Such a script indicates an unsettled and inconsistent inner nature. You never really know how this kind of person will react to a set of circumstances. This writing indicates someone fundamentally insecure who will swing between expression and repression with consummate ease. These mood swings can be easily triggered.

Therefore, people with this kind of handwriting shouldn't be placed in positions of trust for they are ill-disciplined, capricious, and cannot be depended upon to keep calm. While best summed up as being predictably unpredictable, these people can maintain an equilibrium for long periods. However, once they become upset, it is advisable to retire and let them go ahead and express it.

1:2 **Pressure**

Pressure is an indication of the physical and emotional energy present in the writer at the time of writing. Even pressure throughout a sample of writing suggests a good balance between activity and inactivity. If emphasis is placed on something, it is usually on the downward stroke or often at the end of a letter or word.

Heavy pressure People who enjoy activity are more forceful and self-assured than delicate or sensitive people who have a more relaxed outlook on life. Uniformly even but heavier than usual pressure shows vitality and a strong ego. To determine the degree of force behind the writing, lightly touch the back of the paper and you will be able to see and feel it yourself.

If pressure has been emphasized at the end of a letter or word, this writer will be erratic when responding to new situations. It is the handwriting of the ultra-conservative who instinctively opposes anything new, probably because of not understanding the background of a situation or what is involved in it.

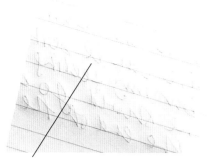

Paper indented by heavy pressure visible on the back of the page

> nalf of all petrol stations ignored Brown's Budget tax cut and kept ncharged, it emergered yesterday.
> g to a survey by the AA, 46 per ce
> then 5,600 stations surveyed b

Even, yet heavy pressure

> Prediction. I have had a
> biorhythms chart from them
> for many years, & would

Light or very light pressure Faint or weak lines imply delicacy of feeling, a sensitive temperament, and someone who is receptive and sympathetic. The writer's nature is yielding and tolerant, but they may suffer from a lack of vitality.

Lettering faint, pressure light

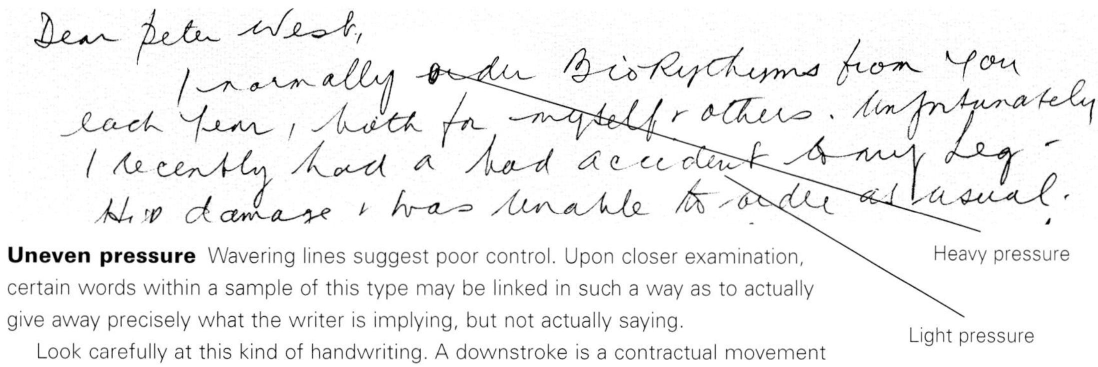

[handwritten sample]

> Dear Peter West,
>   I normally order BioRhythms from you
> each year, both for myself & others. Unfortunately
> I recently had a bad accident to my Leg -
> Hip damage & was unable to order as usual.

Heavy pressure

Light pressure

Uneven pressure Wavering lines suggest poor control. Upon closer examination, certain words within a sample of this type may be linked in such a way as to actually give away precisely what the writer is implying, but not actually saying.

Look carefully at this kind of handwriting. A downstroke is a contractual movement and is often strongly etched. The upstroke shows a release of pressure and may be more lightly made. An unevenness in a writer's script reveals that they are affected by their surroundings and the people in them.

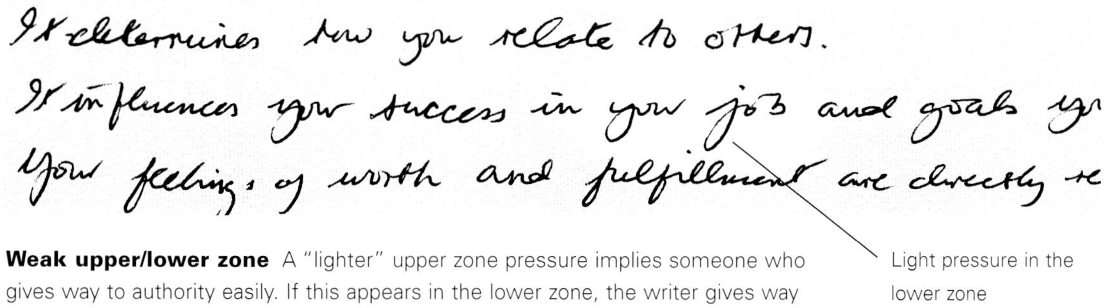

[handwritten sample]

> It determines how you relate to others.
> It influences your success in your job and goals you
> Your feelings of worth and fulfillment are directly re

Light pressure in the lower zone

Weak upper/lower zone A "lighter" upper zone pressure implies someone who gives way to authority easily. If this appears in the lower zone, the writer gives way to instincts.

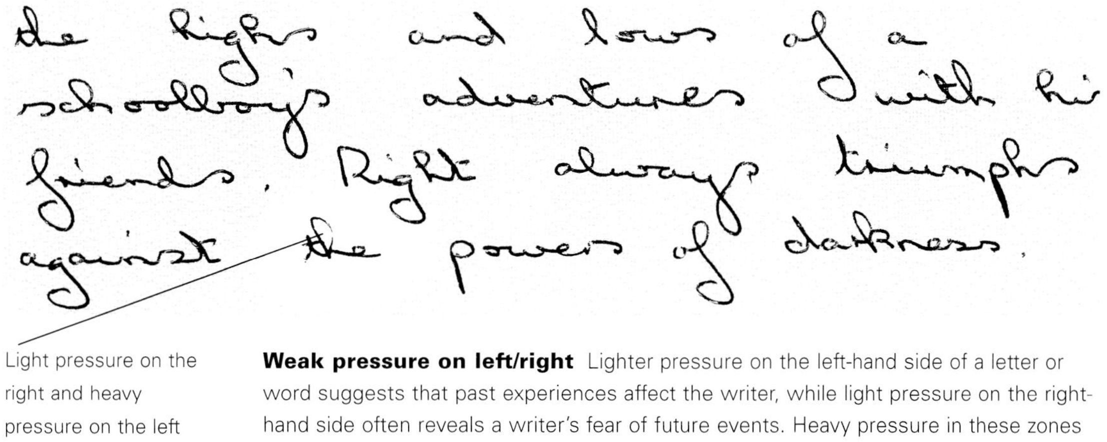

[handwritten sample]

> the highs and lows of a
> schoolboy's adventures I with his
> friends, Right always triumphs
> against the power of darkness.

Light pressure on the right and heavy pressure on the left

Weak pressure on left/right Lighter pressure on the left-hand side of a letter or word suggests that past experiences affect the writer, while light pressure on the right-hand side often reveals a writer's fear of future events. Heavy pressure in these zones will imply opposite effects (▶▶ *Heavy pressure* and *Weak upper/lower zone*).

1:3 Size

USE YOUR TOOLKIT

The way a writer wants to be viewed by others, at work or at play, will be conveyed by the size of the person's handwriting and how it occupies space (▶▶ *Spacing*, pages 20–25; *Margins*, pages 26–29). Most people place great emphasis on this, for they like to think they are well regarded at all times. Of course this is not always so, but the way letters, lines, and words are spaced reveals how they think they may fit in with their environment—although not necessarily how they really do. Their sense of worth and overall self-esteem will be indicated by the size of their letters.

Average script

Generally speaking, a text's middle zone letters are measured for size. The accepted average is around $\frac{1}{8}$ inch (3 mm). Handwriting bigger than this should be reckoned as large script, while anything smaller is small script.

   Those who pen an average- or normal-sized script with little or no variations tend to be practical, realistic, and largely conventional. As a rule, such people fit in well with others because they are adaptable, steady, and reliable. People with normal-sized handwriting know the difference between right and wrong. They tend to get on with their daily tasks without too much fuss.

umhng   and make it as natural   as

possible   It locks authentic enough

Down-to-earth A clear, well-proportioned handwriting style indicates a person one usually can trust to do the right thing at the right time.

Average-size handwriting

Large script

People who use large script are expressing an inner need to be recognized and make an impression. They try to be in the middle of everything and flourish best only when they are the center of attention. Often they dislike their own company, and some will go out of their way to be with other people as much as possible. Large writing reveals an expansive nature and an inability to concentrate for any length of time.

   Writers of large script can display a selfish nature. They may be restless and lack discipline. Also, they can exhibit a tendency to embellish the truth. However, on the plus side, they tend to have a little more optimism than most people.

Vanitas vanitatum, omnis vanitas

Impetuous Large handwriting suggests impatience, poor self-discipline, and someone who does not always think things through before acting.

Larger-than-average script

Small script

People who write small tend to be shy, although not necessarily retiring. When the need arises, they will concentrate hard for long periods of time. They have the capacity to handle facts and figures with the attention to detail necessary for work where such things are of foremost importance. Although they are loyal employees and employers, and make good, reliable friends, they can be quite independent in their ways.

They enjoy playing and working behind-the-scenes; the limelight rarely appeals much to them. In many cases, they have a very strong and calculating inner drive, a trait that marks them for executive positions.

Careful Small written letters are always a sign of reserve, and of someone fairly modest who tends to rely more on facts than on ideas.

magns est veritas et prsevalet

Small script

Variable size script

Those who pen a script with letters that vary in size are emotionally off-balance a lot of the time. They cannot always concentrate and are often moody and self-centered, with changeable ideas and opinions. Without ascertaining all the facts, they respond rapidly to the mood of the moment and readily play the skeptical lawyer or devil's advocate. These people are likely to wear their emotions on their sleeves and are often demonstrative in a physical sense. If rebuffed, they can display childish tendencies.

Careless Variable letters within handwritten matter show indecision, restlessness, and a certain amount of selfishness in their writer.

albo lapillo notare diem

Inconsistent letter size

1:4 **Spacing**

USE YOUR TOOLKIT

The amount of space writers leave between letters, words, and lines indicates their general companionableness, how they react in close personal associations and in relation to their overall environment (▶▶ *Margins, pages 26–29 for other tips on spacing indications).* How they employ the space available on a page will indicate their level of consistency, organizational skills, and personal restraint or tolerance. It also indicates whether they are narrow- or broad-minded.

Letter spacing

The amount of space between letters reveals writers' true thoughts, and how they feel about and relate to people around them at work and leisure. Extroverts leave a lot of space, while introverts keep a tight grip on the size of the gap they create.

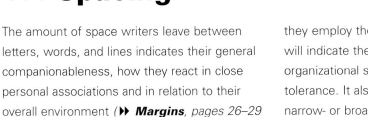

Extrovert

Introvert

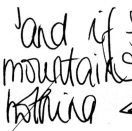

Squeezed letters

Tightly spaced letters Writers whose letters appear squeezed together, so that some or all letters look slightly taller than wide, can and do enjoy close relationships but may be unable to express their inner emotional natures.

Evenly spaced letters Moderately spaced letters show a good sense for social niceties. People with this kind of handwriting mix easily and get along with others very well when they put their minds to it. They know how to stand on their own feet and are usually able to cope with most situations.

Barbecue d'intérieur ou le cuisson est un moyen

Even spacing between letters

comments you had made about hers

Widely spaced wide letters Written matter where each letter appears to be wide, and the space between letters is also wide, indicates that its composer has an outgoing, extroverted character. In such people, extravagance is likely. They revel when they are the center of attention, as they love to be noticed.

Wide gaps between words, and some wide letters

was a need for a moment of absolute honesty that eventually allowed him to realise that his

Widely spaced narrow letters Cautious people tend to pen a script that looks cramped and closed in. Authors of writing that is narrow but has wide gaps between words will be fairly easygoing and generous on the surface, but inwardly they will be reserved and emotionally cautious.

Slightly cramped letters but with wide spacing between words

Wide writing with narrow spacing between letters

the earliest examples of women's writ Vindolanda - a Roman fort in North writing is in Latin and is written

Narrowly spaced wide letters Writers whose letter formations are wide but have narrow gaps between them will show outward signs of selfishness. However, they will generally allow others more latitude than themselves despite their self-centeredness.

A simple assessment method

One of the easiest ways to judge the breadth or width of handwriting is to measure the lower-case version of the letter "n." In normal script, this letter should look almost square in appearance. When writing is cramped, it will look narrow and be badly formed. In a broad script, the letter will appear extended.

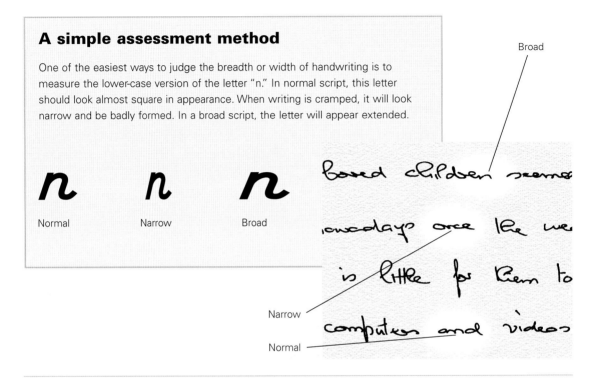

Normal   Narrow   Broad

Broad

Narrow

Normal

Word spacing

Gaps that writers leave between words is a sign of how well they relate to others. The size of the gap also shows how advanced a person's social abilities are.

Narrow script with some overlapping

Narrow gaps Writers of handwriting where spaces between words seem narrow, or even overlap in places, are selfish, and will be at the forefront of everything all the time. They will always want a degree of personal independence.

Average gaps Average gaps between words show good social sense. Authors of these will have independent characters and give as good as they get with others.

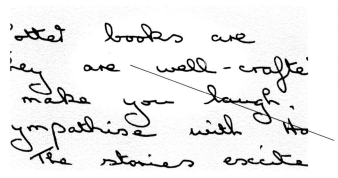

credo quia absurdam est

cuius regio eius religio

albo kapillo notare diem

Moderate spacing

Wide gaps Very wide spaces between words are a clear indication that the writer must have privacy—at all times. Some writers with this habit can be very difficult people to approach and may seem aloof, as they are liable to act without any restraint or respect for rules.

'otter books are
they are well-crafte'
make you laugh.
ympathise with the
The stories excite

Wide spacing
between words

me 12 months Bionythms
biograms. I enclose a cheque for £5.
My date of birth is 6 November 1952.
Many thanks and best wishes.

Inconsistent letters
and gaps

Variable letter size and spacing When handwriting exhibits variable letter sizes (▶ *Size*, pages 18–19) and spacing, it shows an inner nature that is off-balance a lot of the time. Writers of this sort blow hot and cold, are inconsistent in their responses, and frequently quite selfish. More often than not, they are moody, and one can never be certain how they will react to anything. All of this suggests immaturity but, despite these failings, such writers often prove to be good companions.

Line spacing

The amount of space that writers leave between lines will show how much they like to keep themselves to themselves. If they prefer to distance themselves from the rest of society, or even family members in some cases, it may be distinguished by how they organize space on a page.

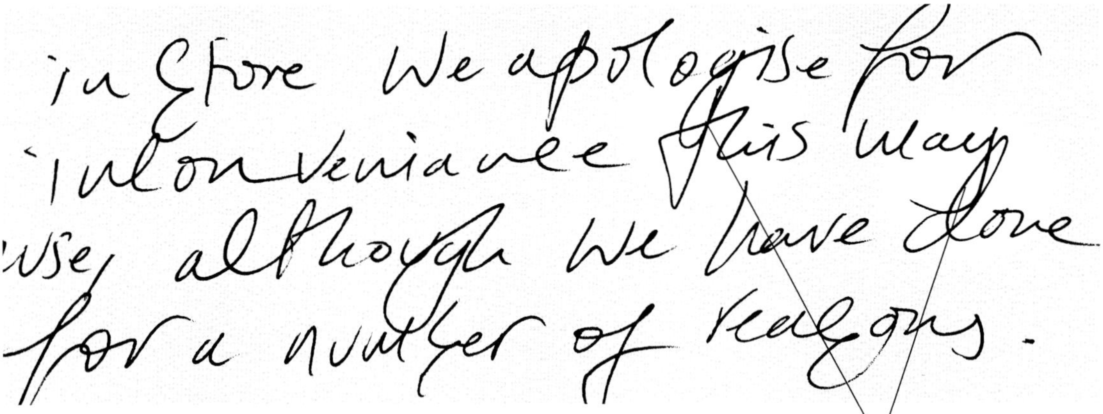

[handwriting sample]

Tight line spacing with entangled loops A character riddled with self-doubt and inner confusion but a fondness for social intercourse is indicated when the upper loops of letters in one line reach high enough to tangle with the lower loops of those in the line above, or even into its middle zone. The thinking of such writers is confused. When challenged, they are often defensive or self-protective. They are likely to blame everyone but themselves for whatever may have failed, even when something is obviously their fault. They often lack organizational skills. If the upper and lower loops of lines are entangled throughout their writing, there may be some unlived or unresolved sexual fantasy present.

Muddled lines

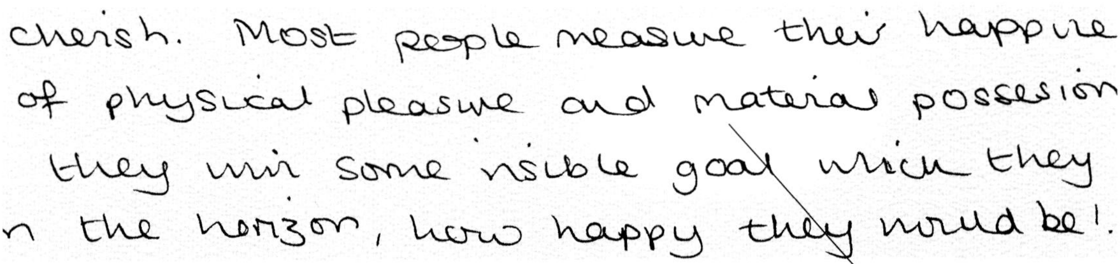

[handwriting sample]

Very regular line spacing Extremely regular spacing between lines is always a sign of the control freak. These are people who dislike losing control of themselves or of circumstances within their environment. Because of this, they may lack common sense.

Wide spaces and a little too regular

Please forwardci a graphology analy the enclosed speciman.

A cheque for £tt togather with Stamped addressed envelope is also

Wide line spacing The wider the spacing between lines, the more writers prefer to be isolated from people. They dislike being close to others and must have privacy. Not wanting, or perhaps even fearing, close contact they set themselves apart, perhaps in the belief that they are better than the people around them. Often people like this have been hurt in the past, finding it difficult to forget.

Lines set well apart

- alor ce soir.— c'est mon Anné Sur je suis supa hemeux d'av emis ici autour de la table, con ellum nous casser le ventre av ~ petits plats.

Irregular line spacing Irregular spacing between lines is always a sign of poor control and shows the writer's lack of organization. These people may also lack common sense.

Variations in line spacing

1:5 **Margins**

USE YOUR TOOLKIT

The way writers work within a page, and particularly how they form and work within margins, will indicate a variety of characteristics. These characteristics may be emphasized by the style of handwriting, and its slant, slope, and lead-in strokes (▶▶ *Slant*, *pages 12–15;* **Line slope**, *pages 42–43;* **Lead-in strokes**, *pages* 56–57). Good writing with poorly planned margins means something quite different from low-level script featuring good margins. Check for pressure, speed, and spacing in the handwriting before making a final analysis (▶▶ **Pressure**, *pages 16–17;* **Speed**, *page 44–45;* **Spacing**, *pages 20–25).*

Narrow margins Small or nonexistent margins indicate a writer who does not plan well and may not communicate effectively. Such a person may alternate between being generous one minute and miserly the next.

Lorem ipsum, Dolor sit amet, consectetuer adipiscing elit, sed diam nonummy nibh euismod tincidunt ut laoreet dolore magna aliquam erat volutpat. Ut wisi enim ad minim veniam, quis nostrud exerci tation ullamcorper suscipit lobortis nisl ut aliquip ex ea commodo consequat. Duis autem vel eum iriure dolor in hendrerit in vulputate velit esse molestie consequat, vel illum dolore eu feugiat nulla facilisis at vero eros et accumsan et iusto odio dignissim qui blandit praesent luptatum zzril delenit augue duis dolore te feugait nulla facilis

Lorem ipsum, Dolor sit amet, consectetuer adipiscing elit, sed diam nonummy nibh euismod tincidunt ut laoreet dolore magna aliquam erat volutpat. Ut wisi enim ad minim veniam, quis nostrud exerci tation ullamcorper suscipit lobortis nisl ut aliquip ex ea commodo consequat.

Wide margins Someone who writes with wide margins cannot or does not quite "fit in" and may be unpopular for not giving proper consideration to the niceties of social life.

Wide left-hand margin A wide left-hand margin indicates someone who needs to feel wanted, may be over-friendly, and likes to live lavishly. This person can appear distant or reserved and is not easy to get along with.

Lorem ipsum, Dolor sit amet, consectetuer adipiscing elit, sed diam nonummy nibh euismod tincidunt ut laoreet dolore magna aliquam erat volutpat. Ut wisi enim ad minim veniam, quis nostrud exerci tation ullamcorper suscipit lobortis nisl ut aliquip ex ea commodo consequat. Duis autem vel eum iriure dolor in hendrerit in vulputate velit esse molestie consequat, vel illum dolore eu feugiat nulla nulla facilisi.

Narrow left-hand margin This writer may not be very popular and could exhibit poor taste socially. Personal security will be important to this person, who may have had a difficult upbringing.

Lorem ipsum,
Dolor sit amet, consectetuer
adipiscing elit, sed diam nonummy
nibh euismod tincidunt ut laoreet
dolore magna aliquam erat
volutpat. Ut wisi enim ad minim
veniam, quis nostrud exerci tation
ullamcorper suscipit lobortis nisl ut
aliquip ex ea commodo consequat.
Duis autem vel eum iriure dolor in
hendrerit in vulputate velit esse
molestie consequat, vel illum dolore
eu feugiat nulla facilisis at vero.

Lorem ipsum,
Dolor sit amet, consectetuer
adipiscing elit, sed diam nonummy
nibh euismod tincidunt ut laoreet
dolore magna aliquam erat
volutpat. Ut wisi enim ad minim
veniam, quis nostrud exerci tation
ullamcorper suscipit lobortis nisl
ut aliquip ex ea commodo
consequat. Duis autem vel
eum iriure dolor in hendrerit in
vulputate velit esse molestie
consequat, vel illum dolore eu
feugiat nulla facilisi vero.

Widening left-hand margin When this margin progressively widens, enthusiasm and impulsiveness will be evident. The writer needs independence and is ambitious but may be unable to organize or plan effectively. This is also a clear indication of fast handwriting (▶▶ ***Speed***, *pages 44–45*).

Narrowing left-hand margin When the left-hand margin narrows, the writer cannot let go of the past and may be cautious or unable to trust anyone. This person also may tire easily and lack confidence.

Lorem ipsum,
Dolor sit amet, consectetuer
adipiscing elit, sed diam
nonummy nibh euismod
tincidunt ut laoreet dolore
magna aliquam erat volutpat.
Ut wisi enim ad minim
veniam, quis nostrud exerci
tation ullamcorper suscipit
lobortis nisl ut aliquip ex ea
commodo consequat. Duis
autem vel eum iriure dolor in
hendrerit in vulputate velit esse
molestie consequat, vel illum
dolore eu feugiat nulla facilisis
at vero.

Lorem ipsum,
Dolor sit amet, consectetuer
adipiscing elit, sed diam nonummy
nibh euismod tincidunt ut laoreet
dolore magna aliquam erat volutpat.
Ut wisi enim ad minim veniam, quis
nostrud exerci tation ullamcorper
suscipit lobortis nisl ut aliquip ex ea
commodo consequat. Duis autem vel
eum iriure dolor in hendrerit in vulputate
velit esse molestie consequat, vel illum
dolore eu feugiat nulla facilisis at vero.

Wide right-hand margin A wide right-hand margin indicates someone who fears the future and is sensitive and reserved. This person can be self-conscious, restless, and pessimistic, which makes partnerships difficult to make and maintain.

Narrow right-hand margin This writer looks forward rather than back to the past and is socially active, but can be accident-prone, and may lack common sense at times.

Lorem ipsum,
Dolor sit amet, consectetuer
adipiscing elit, sed diam nonummy
nibh euismod tincidunt ut laoreet
dolore magna aliquam erat volutpat.
Ut wisi enim ad minim veniam, quis
nostrud exerci tation ullamcorper
suscipit lobortis nisl ut aliquip ex ea
commodo consequat. Duis autem vel eum
iriure dolor in hendrerit in vulputate velit
esse molestie consequat, vel et iusto odio
dignissim qui blandit praesent zzril delenit
augue duis dolore te feugait nulla facilisi.

Lorem ipsum,
Dolor sit amet, consectetuer adipiscing elit, sed
diam nonummy nibh euismod tincidunt ut
laoreet dolore magna aliquam erat volutpat.
Ut wisi enim ad minim veniam, quis nostrud
exerci tation ullamcorper suscipit lobortis nisl
ut aliquip ex ea commodo consequat. Duis
autem vel eum iriure dolor in hendrerit in
vulputate velit esse molestie consequat, vel et
iusto odio dignissim qui blandit praesent zzril
delenit augue duis dolore te feugait nulla
facilisi.

Narrowing right-hand margin A margin of this kind is a sign of a shy, reserved person whose self-confidence is weak. This writer is usually afraid of the future and other people.

Lorem Ipsum,
Dolor sit amet, consectetuer adipiscing
elit, sed diam nonummy nibh euismod
tincidunt ut laoreet dolore magna
aliquam erat volutpat. Ut wisi enim ad
minim veniam, quis nostrud exerci
tation ullamcorper suscipit lobortis
nisl ut aliquip ex ea commodo
consequat. Duis autem vel eum
iriure dolor in hendrerit in
vulputate velit esse molestie
consequat, vel et iusto odio
dignissim qui blandit praesent
zzril delenit augue duis dolore te
feugait nulla facilisi.

Widening right-hand margin Someone who means well to start with but whose impulses soon take over is indicated by this margin. Naturally friendly and easy to get along with, this person may dislike early familiarity and exhibit initial shyness that vanishes early.

Lorem ipsum,
Dolor sit amet, consectetuer
adipiscing elit, sed diam nonummy
nibh euismod tincidunt ut laoreet
dolore magna aliquam erat
volutpat. Ut wisi enim ad
minim veniam, quis nostrud exerci
tation ullamcorper suscipit lobortis
nisl ut aliquip ex ea commodo
consequat. Duis autem vel eum iriure
dolor in hendrerit in vulputate velit
esse molestie consequat, vel et iusto
odio dignissim qui blandit praesent
zzril delenit augue duis dolore te
feugait nulla facilisi.

Uneven left and right margins Anyone who writes with both margins uneven may display defiant moments or rebelliousness and can be unreliable, living as moods dictate. An uneven left-hand margin indicates poor self-control and, sometimes, a lack of initiative. An uneven right-hand margin is more common. If it occurs because of grammar, some sign of control in the person is indicated; if not, the writer is demonstrating poor planning ability and judgment.

Lorem ipsum,
Dolor sit amet, consectetuer
adipiscing elit, sed diam nonummy
nibh euismod tincidunt ut laoreet
dolore magna aliquam erat volutpat.
Ut wisi enim ad minim veniam, quis
nostrud exerci tation ullamcorper
suscipit lobortis nisl ut aliquip ex ea
commodo consequat. Duis autem vel
eum iriure dolor in hendrerit in
vulputate velit esse molestie .

Wide base margin A wide base margin usually indicates reserve and caution, especially in close emotional relationships that may involve sex. The writer will be something of an idealist and not very easy to get to know.

Lorem ipsum,
Dolor sit amet, consectetuer adipiscing
elit, sed diam nonummy nibh euismod
tincidunt ut laoreet dolore magna
aliquam erat volutpat. Ut wisi enim
ad minim veniam, quis nostrud exerci
tation ullamcorper suscipit lobortis nisl
ut aliquip ex ea commodo consequat.
Duis autem vel eum iriure dolor in
hendrerit in vulputate velit esse
molestie consequat, vel illum dolore eu
feugiat nulla facilisis at vero. Lorem
ipsum dolor sit amet, consectetuer
adipiscing elit, sed diam nonummy
nibh euismod tincidunt ut laoreet
dolore magna aliquam erat volutpat.

Narrow base margin A narrow base margin suggests materialism. Physical activity is probable and the writer may be a collector. Sensuality and selfishness are also indicated.

Lorem ipsum,
Dolor sit amet, consectetuer adipiscing
elit, sed diam nonummy nibh euismod
tincidunt ut laoreet dolore magna
aliquam erat volutpat. Ut wisi enim ad
minim veniam, quis nostrud exerci tation
ullamcorper suscipit lobortis nisl ut
aliquip ex ea commodo consequat. Duis
autem vel eum iriure dolor in hendrerit in
vulputate velit esse molestie consequat, vel
illum dolore eu feugiat nulla facilisis at
vero.

Wide top margin This used to be taught in schools as a traditional mark of respect and is recognized as the manner in which letters should be headed. It implies modesty on behalf of the writer.

Lorem ipsum,
Dolor sit amet, consectetuer
adipiscing elit, sed diam nonummy
nibh euismod tincidunt ut laoreet
dolore magna aliquam erat volutpat.
Ut wisi enim ad minim veniam, quis
nostrud exerci tation ullamcorper
suscipit lobortis nisl ut aliquip ex ea
commodo consequat. Duis autem
vel eum iriure dolor in hendrerit in
vulputate velit esse molestie
consequat, vel illum dolore eu
feugiat nulla facilisis at vero.

Narrow top margin This kind of margin indicates a lack of respect on the part of the writer, and also poor planning and a lack of common courtesy. Its author may be too informal and could be aggressive.

In-depth Analysis: *Thank-you letter*

Jennifer is an outgoing young lady who gets along with most people. She is an affable type, sociable, and usually willing to go along with the majority in a group. This thank-you note she has penned to Archie is not representative of her normal outgoing nature. In fact, if anything, it is slightly stilted when compared to her usual approach to people. She has employed all three slants in her response and even her baseline is not very even.

Overall, her writing suggests that, when she wrote this, she was slightly off-balance emotionally. Possibly the gift she received from Archie was not something she wanted. As this is the point of the whole exercise, we may assume she means to say thank-you. However, it is clear she is unhappy with the gift.

This "t" is different from the others suggesting a lack of honesty

2

Jurt

Dear

1

Jurt

Letters separate from the rest of the word and slanting away, such as this "D" and "J," show an element of reluctance

3

junifer

winter

Dear Archie,

Just a quick note to thank you for the lovely jumper you sent you my birthday. Now the winter is here again I'm sure it will get a lot of use!

I hope you are well and keeping busy,

lots of love from

Jennifer.
X

4 **Frequently changing slant** indicates that the writer is not happy

A "potlid p" shows a willful nature with a hint of dishonesty

Underlined signature with a period marks a final emphasis on the message

The signature placed a long way below the message means that the writer does not wish to be associated with what may not be entirely the truth

Analysis

1 The "D" of "Dear" and the "J" of "Just" both stand apart and are at different angles from the rest of the word in which they appear. These and their reclined slant suggest a reluctance to join in or conform.

2 The letter "t" of the word "just" suggests an economy with the truth. Later in the same line, Jennifer has used a forward slant for the word "thank," while "you" and "for" are both stepped up, thus emphasizing the issue.

3 A "jumper" is a British term for a sweater. The word has been written with a slight backward slope and is part of an uneven baseline.

4 The whole third line switches first one way, and then the other, indicating that she is unhappy. At the end, she employs an exclamation mark to emphasize the suggestion that she is sure the jumper will get a lot of use. Perhaps she should have said "it will" rather than "I am sure."

5 Tongue-in-cheek, she hopes he (Archie) is in good health and keeping busy. The "potlid p", with the open base in the middle zone, shows a willful nature with a hint of dishonesty. The truth is, she couldn't care less. She probably hopes that he is keeping busy and therefore won't be able to find the time to bother her again, for a little while at least.

6 Her signature has been underlined, ends with a period, and has been placed a long way away from the message. The underline marks an emphasis on the message, while the period shows that she wants this to be the last word on the subject.

7 When a signature is placed at a significant distance away from the last line of a message, it shows the writer is not entirely happy with what has been written. It means that the writer does not wish to be associated with what may not be entirely the truth.

HOW CAN YOU TELL IF SOMEONE IS REALLY GRATEFUL? LOOK FOR:

▸ No loops in the letter "d"

▸ Closed tops to "a" and "o" letters

▸ A fairly fast speed with a distinct slant to the right

▸ A steady pressure

▸ An even baseline

▸ Signature ought to be the same size as the rest of the missive

▸ Equal size letters and spacing between letters, words, and lines.

Chapter 2

Emotions and Feelings

Our handwriting reflects our state of mind and emotional balance at the time we put pen to paper. This chapter reveals a writer's inner emotions by examining the way loops are formed, line slope, and the speed of writing. The four main styles of writing are discussed as further evidence of emotional characteristics.

2:1 **Loops**

USE YOUR TOOLKIT

A loop, no matter where it appears, is always a sign of emotion. A stroke made where a loop might be expected to be seen is a sure indication of emotional guardedness. Examine these strokes carefully to determine the extent of emotional expression or repression in their authors.

Do remember that the manner with which writers make connections between letters shows their level of inspiration, intuition, and logic. However, strictly speaking, this is better dealt with later in this chapter (▶▶ *Four distinct styles*, pages 46–47).

ASSESSING LOOPS

The amount of emotion writers display is measured by the height, width, and depth a loop makes in relation to the zone in which it appears. An angular appearance suggests a certain amount of aggression, while the rounder it is, the more submissive the writer's nature. Any loop made with a point at the tip of an ascender or the base of a descender shows a hint of rebelliousness and temper, someone who cannot quite conform. A pointed upper loop will indicate someone who thinks for him- or herself.

Upper zone

Middle zone

Lower zone

Upper zone loops

The upper zone represents imaginative and intellectual abilities. Loops here reveal not only writers' intellectual prowess but also how much emotion may be involved in how they make decisions and put them into practice.

Wide loop A wide upper loop implies an ability to take center stage and entertain people.

Expansive loop on the "d"

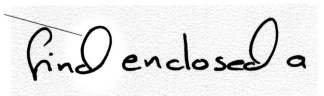

Tall loop   When a loop seems unusually high in proportion to the rest of the script, it implies a visionary nature. Often accompanying this is a lack of practicality; common sense succumbs to imagination.

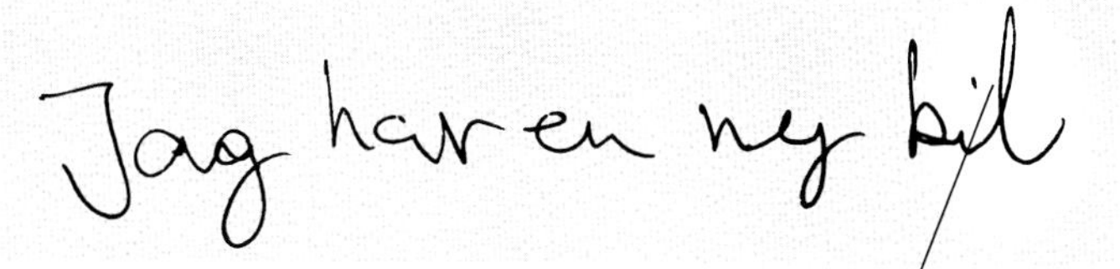

Unusually high ascender loop

An "I" so high and wide that it crashes into letter above

High and wide loop   A high, wide loop with a slightly square appearance shows aggression. This is a writer who has a rather firm or rigid attitude in his or her dealings with others.

Exaggerated loop   Any loop that is exaggerated suggests the writer tends to go along with everyone and everything while keeping real feelings pent up inside. However, the display of temper that occurs when the person loses equilibrium can be quite significant.

Exaggerated loop

Retraced loop

Retraced loop   A retraced loop implies inhibition or repression. This is someone unable or unwilling to properly express emotional responses, who does not allow anyone to get too close, and may seem formal or aloof.

Balloon loop may occur on the "h"

Balloon loop A balloon-like loop at the top of a letter, especially the "h," indicates humor with originality of thought and ideas. Narrow script in the middle zone with this style of loop suggests the writer may be narrow-minded.

Narrow loop
Repression or hidden worries are behind narrow loops. The writer dreams and fantasizes with little practical follow-up.

Narrow loop on ascenders

Broken loop appears on the upper stroke

Broken loop A broken upper loop is usually made with a break on the upper stroke. Its writer may be experiencing anxiety and unnecessary worry, and will be uncertain regarding abilities, feelings, ideals, or relationships. If the break is made on a down stroke, there may be a physical or mental disorder in the writer, but only at the time of writing.

Small loop Loops small in proportion to the size of handwriting suggests a practical, down-to-earth approach to life. While reliable and able to get the job done, such a writer will lack ambition.

Small loops on large script

Lower zone loops

The lower zone is where you look to uncover the basic or physical side of someone's inner nature. It is here that people tend to reveal their natural inclinations.

Loops should be properly shaped and look as though they "belong" to the rest of the script. This shows a balanced, healthy person with average drives and instincts.

Wide or triangular loop

Triangular or wide loops are an indication of exaggeration and inner discord, suggesting an element of impulsiveness and aggression in the writer. This person may dislike change.

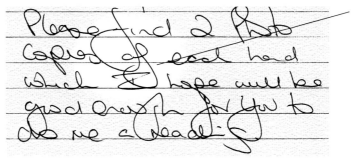

Wide loop on letter "g"

Variable loops A variety of loops shows a colorful imagination. The more there are, the more extreme it will be. Frequent mood changes attend this personality. Loops that are distorted reflect an emotionally disturbed inner nature. The rest of the script may provide clues to the probable cause for this.

Range of loops

Long oval loop A long oval loop indicates basic, earthy physical drives, someone who likes to achieve and prides himself on acquisition and possession. The writer almost always has a strong libido.

Long and round, butts into script line below

No loops A stroke or line where a loop should be is a sign of emotional repression. This signifies a writer who has adopted a controlled mental approach to emotional responses.

Absence of loops

mite right-handed while I still do

'o' I do other things left handed

Loop peters out

Ragged loop Irrespective of size, when a loop appears broken or ragged, it can mean something is wrong with the writer's physical health. It may be something temporary, like a broken lower limb or a temporary loss of its use.

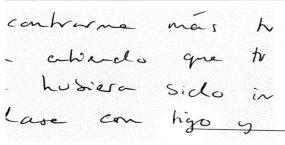

contrarme más h

— cuando que tv

hubiera sido in

Lase con tigo y

Squat, short loop

Small loop Small loops that do not reach down very far imply sexual inadequacy or other, similar problems. The writer's general health will be weak, with an attendant lack of stamina and vitality.

Open loop The open or unfinished loop that swings wide to the left is a sign of an impressionable mind and is often seen in the handwriting of young adolescents. In older writers, it shows an unsatisfactory sex life; the smaller the cradle, the more this will be so.

ting which system
usually based on the
each individual

Open loop swinging wide

Cradle loop Loops that swing toward the left imply that the writer has problems trying to forget earlier emotional problems. They want to hold on to the past and have trouble maintaining a relationship with a current partner because of this. They can be very sensitive souls.

albae gallinae f

Cradle loop

Right-swing loop Loops that pull forward and to the right show people who channel both their emotional and physical energies into practical activities, perhaps while following their ambitions. These people are easily stimulated and are likely to wear their hearts on their sleeves.

Right-swing loop

Claw loop Lower loops sometimes reach downward, then swing up and to the left like a small claw. This suggests a dislike of responsibility; the writer needs someone else to be in control. Greed and selfishness may also be traits.

Descender reaches down before curving upward

Double loop The double loop indicates the worrier who is unable to let go even when a matter is fully resolved. This writer can be negatively compulsive and over-persistent to the point of embarrassment.

Noticeable double loop

Exaggerated loop Exaggerated lower loops are a sign of restlessness, or an active type who flourishes best in company because of the stimulation it brings. Such writers' drives push them on and they can have trouble identifying their needs.

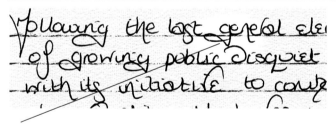

Exaggerated loops reaching far down into the lower zone

Middle zone loops

Loops should not be seen anywhere within the middle zone. No letters are formally created with them. However, there are occasions when a loop is made in this zone, often inside the letters "a," "e," and "o." Sometimes they also appear in the middle zone formation of the letters "d," "g," "p," and "y."

In graphology, a loop represents emotion. When it is made where it should not occur, the writer may be emotionally sensitive but unable to express his or her feelings. Such people can exhibit a defensive manner; at times they may be aggressive. To determine how this will be directed or manifest, examine the rest of their script.

stop

Sun was so near the ground, and vard so flat, that the shadows are and Tess would stretch a of a mile ahead of them, like gers pointing afar to where the

Loop at top of oval   Loop on left of oval

Small loop at top of letter When the letters "a" and "o" are written with a small loop at the top left, top right, or even both sides at the same time, their writers can be trusted with secrets. However, they may not be entirely honest with themselves or others regarding what they say or do.

Loop on left side of letter A loop on the left-hand side of a letter suggests discretion. This is someone who will keep a secret and handle awkward moments with diplomacy and tact.

Loop on right side of letter If a loop occurs on the right-hand side of a middle zone letter, its writer has an open and friendly approach, but can be careless. This is someone who does not intend harm, but just does not always stop and think.

Loop on right side
in middle zone

for some 'year now I have going through some quite de smooth emotionaller, and am

Double loop on an oval

Double loops on an oval Writers of the double loop are inclined to deceive themselves and others, but not necessarily dishonestly. They cannot always gauge their limitations, and can promise and then fail to do something because they think they are unable to do it.

(ive and unrehearsed was great fun and although it was quite tiring. everyone had a good time.

Stem "d" loop

Loop on letter "d" stem A loop sometimes forms the stem of the letter "d" and this is always a sign of someone sensitive to criticism. This person worries too much about what others think. The bigger the loop, the more this is emphasized. A square appearance to the top of the loop is a sign of aggression and obstinacy.

Loop on letter "t" stem When a loop forms the stem of the letter "t," its writer lacks confidence and may rely too much on others for support. This is someone who does well as long as a steady flow of praise comes their way. A "please" or a "thank-you" will work wonders on such a person. If a bar is not made across a looped stem, the writer is hypersensitive and unable to reason things through properly.

Loop on "t" stem

Liste Courses.
Fruits
Légumes
Pâtes

2:2 **Line slope**

USE YOUR TOOLKIT

Handwriting should normally be created in an even line across a page. At the end of the line, the writer stops, lifts the pen, starts again immediately below that line, and keeps going until the sentence or paragraph is complete. This line should hold relatively steady across the page. When it does, it shows the writer has good self-control. Usually reliable, even-tempered, and well organized, writers of this kind tend to take life in their stride. Their writing suggests they have even, balanced responses to external influences. They can control their moods and, in the event of adversity, maintain equilibrium. Still, they, as do all writers, will display a certain amount of variability in their line slope (▸▸ *Slant*, pages 12–15).

ASSESSING LINE SLOPE

There are always a few writers who experience some degree of difficulty maintaining an even line across a page, even when they write on lined paper—which is one of the reasons why handwriting analysts ask for samples to be made on unlined paper!

Always look at the end of a letter or message first. We all start well, no matter what a missive may be for, but, as we write, we tend to become more involved with what we want to say and our attention to presentation slips. Often you will see several attempts where writers have tried to return to an initial standard in a piece of writing, but, in the end, their true writing style surfaces.

Very even baseline If lines seem too even, as if a ruler has been used (▸▸ *Spacing*, *Very regular line spacing, page 24*), far too much control is being shown by the writer. This indicates great fear of losing control, so much so that spontaneity is poor. It exhibits narrow-mindedness.

Very straight and regular

Convex lines Sometimes script starts at the baseline but slowly arches upward and then descends back to the line again. Convex lines like this show the writer was enthusiastic and confident at the beginning of the exercise, but has tired and may not even finish what has been started.

Script arches upward

Concave lines The opposite of convex is concave handwriting. A line begins straight but then moves below the baseline, eventually rising again at the end. It shows a writer with confidence at the start, who loses interest or imagines lacking the ability to finish the task, then somewhere afterward regains confidence and finishes the job with a more positive outlook.

veen the mundane plane of king and the realm of the gods / Spirits, which we might call otherworld. When he enters the

Handwriting dips up then down

to observe what different ideas of n . Most people measure their happin ysical pleasure and material possessio y mir some nsible goal which they - horizon, how happy they would be is aift or that circumstance they

Lines moving up and down

Wavy lines Handwriting that crosses the page in a series of wavy lines shows someone with strong responses to external stimuli. Such writers are easily sidetracked and their talents often wasted in exercises that take up unnecessary energies. These people can be unreliable.

Falling lines Lines may be written in a level manner at the beginning, but then gradually fall. This frequently occurs when writers are tired or have been working for long periods without adequate rest.

While tiredness is the most usual reason for lines that slope downward, there are other factors to take into account. Those who write this way may be unwell or downhearted because of an emotional problem, bad news, or a disagreement with someone close.

I am a 30yr old, femal work for a large quarrying co. I have been an avid read for many years and find your - in their content. I am particularly interested I ALISMA Train

Script slopes downward

mir hier einen Notar m und uns beraten lassen ventuell pleich eine Entscde herbeiführen können : .ll das one Bild über

Rising lines When lines rise upward in a regular pattern, it may be a reflection of someone's natural enthusiasm and optimism for what is at hand, or simply a sign of a buoyant mood at the time of writing. Habitual writers of this type like to keep themselves busy even when what they are doing is considered foolhardy by others. Very little gets them down.

Script sloping upward

2:3 **Speed**

From the speed of handwriting, you will be able to assess how well the writer's mind was attuned to what was going on at the time of writing. Complementary observations about legibility and how much pressure has been applied while writing (▶▶ **Pressure**, pages 16–17) are linked with those about speed. Clear, readable handwriting is an indication of confidence and ability to communicate ideas. The speed at which someone writes shows how quickly the writer perceives what is required, along with the level of spontaneity.

Fast writers

The fast writer thinks and decides matters quickly and is organized. Such people are not always conformists, as they have a message to convey.

Fast handwriting showing stretched "t"-bars and "i"-dots, a right slant, and a rising line

Fast writing In fast writing, punctuation (especially commas, "i"-dots, and "t"-bars) often stretch into dash marks. As a rule, fast handwriting tends to slope to the right, while a slower script appears vertical or slightly reclined. A rising line is also a clear sign of speed. Other indications to watch out for are a widening left-hand margin (▶▶ **Margins**, pages 26–29) and a lack of lead-in strokes (▶▶ **Lead-in strokes**, pages 56–57).

Crossing the baseline The speed of a script can cause it to be written slightly above or beneath the accepted baseline. From such writing, you can infer that writers are determined to get their message across at all costs and in spite of readers.

Fast handwriting dipping down below the baseline established at the beginning of the line

Slower writers

Slower writers are more conformist and take their time because they like to digest what is in front of them at all times. They are all too aware that someone else will need to understand what they write, so legibility is high on their agenda. Writers of this type consider the future a little more than their faster counterparts.

Very slow speeds are not often encountered, unless someone is elderly, in frail health, or poorly educated. Sometimes you see someone's pace of writing alter in places. An individual word or words will look as though they have been penned slightly more slowly, which implies that the writer took time to stop and think about what to say.

Slow handwriting indicates writers who have taken time to consider their readers and their reactions to the content of their writing. It also could be a form of outer constraint that comes into play naturally when writers' emotions are aroused. At such times, they tend to emphasize certain words or phrases pertinent to their message.

Slow handwriting

Legibility

It is important for aspiring analysts to remember that good, clear handwriting does not always imply intelligence. It also does not always indicate that such writers are of good character, nor does illegibility mean poor character.

Fast handwriting Most people want to be understood and show this by using readable writing, but legibility and speed do not always go together. When they do, expect to find mental energy, enthusiasm, and perception, for people who write this way can be extroverted and a trifle unreliable. They tend to make avoidable errors as they lack a good eye for detail. Their concentration will waver. However, this may depend on their interest levels.

Fast legible handwriting

Slow handwriting The handwriting of slower-paced individuals brings greater legibility, but sometimes the writing style may not have advanced from the type learned at school. Writers of this kind are neater, steadier, more cautious, and more reliable than faster colleagues. They are usually well organized, and, while not quick thinkers, will be thorough and careful.

Slow legible handwriting

2:4 **Four distinct scripts**

Handwriting reflects writers' emotional attitudes at the time they are writing. As a general rule, most people's ordinary handwriting is fairly well balanced, but when they are disturbed, their standards tend to falter. Variations occur in pressure, speed, and connections between individual letters.

Garland script

Round or curved handwriting may resemble a series of open bowls, as if ready to receive offerings from above. This is called the garland style. Although easily recognizable in its pure state, it can sometimes be hard to differentiate between it and arcade script (see below).

Garland writing usually looks reasonably relaxed. It is simple to write in this style, for it flows gently across a page in either shallow or deep garlands—not unlike the lapping of waves on an ocean shore. The writing itself indicates an open, receptive nature, as though the garland is a bowl into which the experiences of life fall.

Saturday, and thank you again for the help you gave me. Feeling a l

KEY CHARACTERISTICS

▶ *Warm and friendly*
▶ *Gullible*
▶ *Followers, not leaders—they lack motivation or the ability to take control*
▶ *Adaptable, almost always respond to emotional appeals*
▶ *Dislike friction; gentle and submissive*
▶ *Like to feel secure and will avoid unpleasantness if threatened in any way*
▶ *Should they become unbalanced, their writing may appear uneven and even contain some angularity.*

Arcade script

In contrast, arcade handwriting resembles a series of arches offering protection. Arcade handwriting reflects a writer's inner uneasiness and is a style exhibited by people who may appear reserved and formal. It implies an overactive sense of self-preservation.

When such people are disturbed, this style's arch pattern will be accentuated and signs of pressure will be very much in evidence. Writers whose arcades are shallow tend to pretend or scheme to get their own way. They are not domineering but neither will they yield easily. They accept change up to a point, but it has to be gradual—and, moreover, practical.

D dentes e a coca, penteava o :lo e vestia-se rapidamente. a sua parte do dia favoeita, pelos actos de higiene pessoal

KEY CHARACTERISTICS

▶ *Conventional*
▶ *Traditional*
▶ *Independent*
▶ *Cautious*
▶ *Watchful*
▶ *Formal*
▶ *Suspicious*
▶ *Frequently very creative; many are musically inclined.*

Angular script

Angular script is created by a simple up-and-down movement of the pen. In it, there are no curves, or very few, and its appearance is angular. This style always suggests authority and power, and a disciplined attitude. Because the pen moves either up or down, both the writing and its author are careful and controlled.

Loops are always a sign of emotion and do not appear in angular script. It is easy, therefore, for writers of this type to make and apply decisions in a coldly efficient manner at all times. With them, the means does not always justify the end. Angular script represents inflexible, decisive types who tend to hide their feelings in everyday matters. If such writers are thrown off balance, their writing's angularity will be emphasized.

etching are painted on o traditional hand blown an glass to stunning effect. initial design and sampl

KEY CHARACTERISTICS

▸ *Disciplined, efficient*
▸ *Decisive*
▸ *Reliable*
▸ *Careful, controlled*
▸ *Lack the ability to compromise, not very adaptable*
▸ *A determined and unyielding approach to life*
▸ *May lack humor*
▸ *Stubborn.*

Thread script

Thread writing is when script deteriorates into a nearly indecipherable or single-line state. This may also be seen in rounded script.

Not always easy to understand, probably because they rarely have a clear sense of direction or purpose, these people have a talent for "arriving" early, having shown much promise in childhood. As a rule, and in spite of the good education that they may have had, they mean well but do not always explain themselves properly.

This sometimes shapeless style of writing represents someone who tries too hard to be all things to all people. When the person is disturbed, this style becomes more pronounced.

I couldn't actually find any on to send you, so thought I'd just letter, but hopefully it will a bobs about my personality (I'm t

KEY CHARACTERISTICS

▸ *Adaptable, charming, talented*
▸ *Individualistic, rebellious*
▸ *Manipulative, flattering*
▸ *Think and act quickly, but not rashly*
▸ *Impressionable*
▸ *Very sensitive*
▸ *Materialistic*
▸ *Broadminded*
▸ *Creative*
▸ *Opportunistic.*

Mixed styles

Not everything comes in its purest form, and handwriting is no exception. Often, someone's handwriting mixes two basic styles. Its dominant trend offers a clue to the way a writer will behave.

Garland and angular Garland writing with aspects of angularity in it shows that its writer has a good sense of observation alongside an astute and clever mind.

Arcade and thread This style of writing belongs to a persuasive and very perceptive type of person who likes to work behind the scenes. Such people know how to keep a secret.

Angular and thread Angular handwriting often has traces of thread connections within its framework. Writers of this type will be direct, abrupt, and aggressive.

Garland and arcade Garland and arcade writing reveals a very positive personality. The writer is often creative and original.

Garland and thread Generally speaking, those who write this way have poor staying-power, and even poorer concentration levels. Such writers are indecisive and have little resistance, and an often-indulged lazy streak.

Arcade and angular People who combine these styles are difficult to get to know. When you do get to know them, they are equally difficult to understand. They are likely to be very critical, inflexible, and intolerant.

In-depth Analysis: *Lonely heart*

There are several things that do not quite add up in this reply to a singles advertisement, the first of which is the very heavy pressure the female writer has used. This—together with the rather erratic, uneven left-hand margin—suggests a lack of emotional balance and a great deal of misdirected emotional and physical energy.

A wide margin at the top of the page shows modesty and respect

5

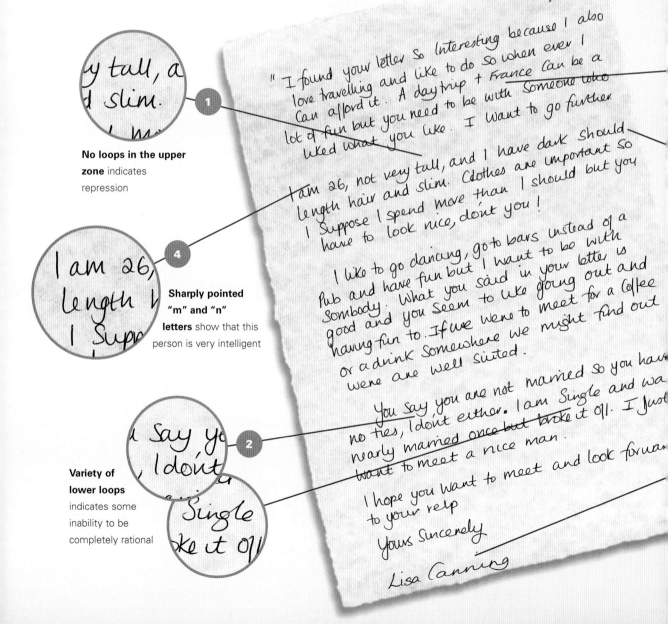

No loops in the upper zone indicates repression

1

4

Sharply pointed "m" and "n" letters show that this person is very intelligent

Variety of lower loops indicates some inability to be completely rational

2

" I found your letter so interesting because I also love travelling and like to do so when ever I can afford it. A day trip + France can be a lot of fun but you need to be with someone who liked what you like. I want to go further.

I am 26, not very tall, and I have dark should length hair and slim. Clothes are important so I suppose I spend more than I should but you have to look nice, don't you!

I like to go dancing, go to bars instead of a pub and have fun but I want to be with somebody. What you said in your letter is good and you seem to like going out and having fun to. If we were to meet for a coffee or a drink somewhere we might find out were are well suited.

You say you are not married so you have no ties, I don't either. I am single and wa nearly married once but broke it off. I just want to meet a nice man.

I hope you want to meet and look forwa to your relp

Yours Sincerely

Lisa Canning

The largely upright script shows that this writer has to fight hard to stay on an even keel emotionally, but if or when something unsettling happens, she will express her feelings spontaneously. In the writing there are indications of repression. She will appear somewhat formal until she feels she can relax.

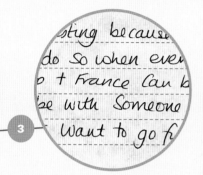

Uneven baselines throughout show an inwardly unsettled character

The signature placed away from the last line shows someone who is distancing themselves from what they have written

The omission of letters indicates a slightly careless nature. Here the word "shoulder" has the "er" at the end missing

Analysis

1 There are no loops in the upper zone at all, but there are a few retraced upper strokes. Her writing is much larger than average and most of it occupies the middle zone—which indicates a writer who lives in the present moment and possibly lacks restraint.

2 Her lower loops are comprised of a variety of tails, which indicate an inconsistency in her approach to everyday matters. This is not excessive, but it does point to some inability to be totally rational. She can be easily sidetracked, especially in her social life.

3 All of her baselines are slightly uneven showing she is flexible in her responses. This also indicates that she has an unsettled character, and can perhaps be moody.

4 Also present are a number of misspelled words or omitted letters. This carelessness shows that she is more concerned with what she wants to say than how she is writing. The speed of her script shows she wants to be well thought of, but actually demonstrates the fact that she is not thinking. This is a shame, because the sharp points of some of her "n" and "m" letters display her quick, perceptive mind.

5 The wide margin at the top of the page implies modesty and respect, and is associated with someone older than she says she is. In addition, she has a very straightforward signature without a period, no special marks, and no underlining. Her signature is placed a little distance away from the last line which suggests that she does not believe all that she has written.

HOW TO TELL WHETHER SOMEONE HAS A GENUINE NATURE

▸ Legible script throughout

▸ Fast speed

▸ Balanced zones

▸ Signature same size as the body of text

▸ An upright script; there may be a slight incline but no more than 10 degrees or so.

Chapter 3

The Public Persona

Take a look at the way the writer relates to the world around them. This chapter discusses how we make an entrance with our capital letters and the significance of lead-in and final strokes. Punctuation, its positioning, and how we dot our "i"s and cross our "t"s are also considered.

3:1 Envelopes

USE YOUR TOOLKIT

Very often, our first impressions of a writer are from the way they have written our name and address on an envelope. Few people pay much attention to how they write an address, beyond making sure it is legible, and yet the way a writer places an address on an envelope reveals much about his or her ego.

Handwriting on an envelope is an important expression of the author's attitude toward other people. For the analyst, it is also an excellent source of capital letters and numbers, being one of those rare places where these are all grouped together.

The script on the outside of an envelope often differs from the style and size of the writing inside. Usually, it is slightly larger because, unconsciously, most people are likely to express their ego here to try to impress. Writing on the envelope that is more or less the same as that of the letter inside shows a well-balanced nature, someone who usually behaves consistently both in public and in private. If the writing on the envelope is smaller than the writing on the missive inside, this suggests false modesty.

If the address is barely legible, the writer has ignored social protocol suggesting a tactless and even rude side to their nature. However, many writers overlook this simple courtesy and may be genuinely unaware of their failure here.

The position of the address on an envelope speaks volumes about the author. An address sited centrally shows proper balance and good judgment. The position of a name and address on the front of an envelope must also be read according to the style, slant, line slope, pressure, and size with which it has been penned.

Ms Marcia Wilson
3 Summer Drive
Orchard Park
MEA 02549-8632
USA.

If the writer places the address toward the top of the envelope, he or she is likely to be a dreamer and an idealist. The author may also lack confidence and the ability to be objective. In addition, this address position does not demonstrate much respect for the addressee.

Juan Vasco
Avda Picasso, 14
Seville E-46034
España

If the writer places the address toward the base of the envelope, he or she will be materialistic, possessive, and impulsive. While reasonably practical, the writer will be somewhat pessimistic. This position is often the sign of a collector.

Helen Middleton
22 High Street
Great Morton
IN50 8GH
England

When the address is written toward the top left-hand side of the envelope, the author will possess an inquiring mind but lack good follow-through, generally because of timidity or a lack of confidence. Such a writer will almost invariably exhibit caution or reserve in the public arena.

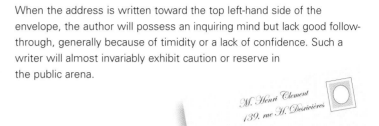

M. Henri Clement
139, rue H. Desrivières
Paris
F-79632

An address placed toward the top right-hand side of the envelope shows carelessness and limited planning ability. This is normally where the stamp should be placed and so this address position shows either a lack of respect for social conventions or plain bad manners.

The writer who pens the address at the bottom half of the envelope and toward the right-hand side demonstrates a straightforward and practical character. This is someone who values their independence immensely—but will, however, rarely challenge social mores.

Petra Schneider
Langenstrasse 3
Bremen D-13462

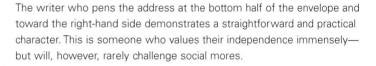

When the name and address are placed at the lower left-hand side of the envelope, the writer reveals a materialistic attitude. He or she has a good memory—little escapes them. However, these people tend to be rather reserved and cautious in their dealings with others.

Mr B. Roland
1250 Graham Ave
San Francisco
CA 94203-9651

The stepped address (one written from around the top half of the envelope through to the bottom right) suggests a conventional nature; someone who has remembered what they were taught at school and has failed to make changes while growing up. Such writers prefer to follow the crowd.

Thomas Wright
6 Cook St
York
YO56 2JG

Underlining a part or all of the name and address with or without a ruler or in a different color ink is rather pointless and shows someone who cannot differentiate between the important and the unimportant. This writer is often stubborn with poor perception and might suffer from compulsiveness. Be aware, however, that underlining addresses is common in some countries.

Anna Olsson
Kungsgatan 22
Lund SE-224 69
Sweden

3:2 **Capital letters**

The way capital letters are written shows the way their writer would like to be viewed by others. They represent the public side of someone's persona. In graphology, a capital letter is evaluated according to its originality, size, and style. An assessment may take two perspectives, with an analysis of the letter in the writer's printed and flowing cursive styles.

CAPITALS INTRODUCE US

Capital letters are symbolic of the way we enter a room or effect an introduction to other people—especially strangers. Like a handshake, a capital letter introduces a writer and, whether we admit it or not, the way we are seen by others is important.

How writers construct capitals shows the level of appreciation and confidence they have in their assessment of their own abilities. A comparison between capital letters and the body of a text reveals a lot about them. This is particularly seen on job applications.

If a piece of writing is directed to a friend, its capitals will show how much value the writer puts on the relationship. When it comes to assessing a love letter, the person receiving it can tell precisely how much their lover really appreciates them.

Assessing capital letters

You should check the start of the letter and note each sentence and paragraph while working through it. If you are looking at correspondence, note the way, and where, the writer has placed the address. In each case, assess letters for consistency or otherwise.

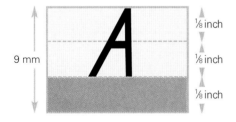

9 mm

⅛ inch

⅛ inch

⅛ inch

Size On average, most capital letters are between ³⁄₁₆–²³⁄₆₄ inch (6–9 mm) tall, since this fits the accepted ⅛ inch (3 mm) size for each writing zone. Anything larger than this is considered large writing. If smaller than this, handwriting is called small. However, unless there is an obvious divergence in these zones, few people pay any attention to the size of their script.

Ornamentation Handwritten capital letters invariably have small markings on them that are quite different from printed versions. Any flourish, additional support stroke, curlicue, loop, or hook suggests the writer is or can be distracted from the matter at hand (▸▸ *Loops*, pages 34–41).

Ornamented capital

Large capital: the "T" is $^{15}/_{32}$ inch (12 mm) high
and the smallest letter is barely $^{5}/_{64}$ inch (2 mm)

Large capitals Any capital letter that appears
extra-large suggests egotism, ambition, vanity, and
probably more than just a hint of insecurity. The writer will
have an extravagant nature with a need to be recognized
at all times.

Generally speaking, capital letters tend to vary slightly
as someone's writing progresses in a text. This is normal
and to be expected.

Small capitals However, a small capital letter
indicates a lack of confidence and ambition, and
poor vitality. It is a sign of someone who prefers to
work in the background. Often this kind of person
makes a good listener and can identify with the
problems of others.

Capital same height as lower case

Misplaced capital appearing in middle of word
shows an unsettled state at the time of
writing; note the other "n" letters

Misplaced capitals While examining the text for these
first letters, look also for capital letters that appear without
reason in the middle of a sentence or a word. Such letters
are always a sure sign of an emotionally impulsive or over-
reactive nature. If they occur in the middle of a word, they
signify temper tantrums and show the writer was in an
unsettled state at the time of writing. If they are placed at
the beginning of a word, this condition is modified
somewhat, but the writer will still have been unsettled
while writing and may practice some form of deception.
Such people may also place too much importance on their
own thoughts and actions, and could even be lying.

Capital separate from rest of word

Isolated capitals The isolated capital letter—that is, one
not linked to the rest of the word of which it is a part—
shows writers who rely too much on their sixth sense. Their
hunches often work, and they may have a lucky touch when
it comes to minor gambling matters. When linked to a word,
a capital shows fluency in a writer's thought. There is little
margin for error for such writers, who like to consider ideas
as much as they can before acting.

3:3 **Lead-in strokes**

USE YOUR TOOLKIT

People tend to hesitate for a brief moment before they finally make up their minds as to precisely what they are going to write. For many, starting to write is easy, but others need a prop of some kind. Like actors about to go on stage, some people feel the need to create a suitable entrance for themselves.

You must remember, however, that certain script systems like the Palmer system, as taught in America, contain lead-in strokes. So be careful to always assess script with reference to the handwriting system.

Most starting strokes, no matter how they are formed or in which zone they appear, suggest an adherence to convention, scholastic teaching, and a certain amount of self-doubt. They show hesitation and a lack of true spontaneity. Writers who use them may be ambitious but will not generally challenge authority without good reason.

Long lead-in strokes Generally speaking, the longer a writer's starting strokes are, the more they are expressing their doubts. Such writers will dislike making, and being seen to make, mistakes. They are conventional, and will probably prefer others to go first, if nothing else other than to learn by their mistakes. They always dislike change.

Long lead-in

No starting stroke The absence of a starting stroke shows a mature, sensible approach to solving problems. These people may not be more intelligent than others, but they often display a strong creative streak. Lack of a lead-in stroke also indicates fast handwriting (▶▶ **Speed**, pages 44-45).

Lack of lead-in stroke

Capital letter lead-in

Capital strokes Lead-in strokes on all capital letters imply show-offs, people who like to emphasize their abilities to suggest they are more gifted than they actually are. They will be overly concerned about their personal appearance.

Upper zone lead-in strokes

Lead-ins made in the upper zone suggest imagination, but not necessarily practicality. They also indicate a writer who makes an effort to be well-prepared in order to demonstrate his or her abilities to others.

Upper zone lead-in

Credo

As well as water and air, we require a constant regular intake of food to provide the major source of energy for movement, breathing, heat regulation, heart function, blood circulation and brainpower.

Middle zone lead-ins

Middle zone lead-in strokes

Middle zone lead-in strokes refer to an ambitious nature and an excess of energy that may be misplaced at times. These writers can be opinionated but do so without malice or intent to upset. While others may see authority or social structures as a challenge, they do not.

ad astra per astra.

Lower zone lead-ins

Lower zone lead-in strokes

Lead-in strokes from the baseline or below are almost always a reminder of problems from the past that still create temporary moments of inner anxiety in the writer. Essentially, this is a writer's prop, something like a child's security blanket, which writers do not really need, yet cannot always do without.

The cause of almost any lead-in stroke from the lower zone will be found in its writer's personal history and may be connected to parental or family disagreements. It may also refer to an inability to make and carry out decisions. As time has gone by, too much self-doubt and uncertainty have built up in the person.

3:4 **Final strokes**

The final stroke of a letter, sentence, or word is the writer's way of saying good-bye and often comes to be recognized almost as widely as the writer's signature. The final stroke contained in a writer's signature is dealt with in the unit on signatures (▶▶ ***Signatures***, *pages 70–75).* Generally, the end stroke offers good clues to the way writers view their future and present social life, and what their general mood of the moment is.

ALTERING NATURAL HANDWRITING

Experience has shown graphologists that final strokes are an excellent point at which to begin forgery investigations. No impulse is so difficult to control as one that must be stopped only to be allowed free movement again immediately afterward. We come to the end of a word, stop, lift the pen slightly, then begin the next word. This single act of handwriting is one of the most difficult acts to copy with any accuracy.

People who naturally write fast find slow handwriting difficult. They are uncomfortable with it in much the same way that slow writers are when they try to hurry. Thus, from the way the end of a line, sentence, or word is written, we may assess its writer's adaptability, habit, and mood according to how they are linked with social conformity and attitudes.

Long final stroke The final stroke that swings outward and upward shows activity, drive, and enthusiasm and, if overly long, implies tenacity. When the end stroke curves up and over the last letter or word, expect to find a self-defensive and self-protective attitude. This attitude will be exaggerated when the whole final word is covered, and such a writer is likely to go to extremes to stay out of trouble.

Strokes swing outward and upward

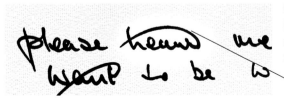

Stroke through a word An end stroke that strikes back through the last word indicates a rather self-destructive nature, and someone who is introverted, negative, and untrusting.

End strokes scores through word

Unfinished final letter Any final letter left unfinished shows its writer's manners leave a lot to be desired. Such people may be rude, argumentative, and brusque. They have little regard for the niceties of social obligations. If this ending has hooks and ticks attached to it, its writer will be possessive and critical. A garlanded type of end stroke eases this somewhat, while the arcade version indicates writers who are more secretive, especially regarding their personal lives. The angular type of end stroke suggests a little more discipline in the character, while a thready style suggests someone who makes too many mistakes because they lack attention to detail.

C'est un trou de ve
Accrochant follement au
D'argent; où le role

Abrupt endings

Swinging end stroke End strokes are sometimes seen to swing down and under the last letter or whole word. This is a sign of materialism and selfishness, and writers who do this may feel uncomfortable with company or in social affairs. They will seem confident and poised socially, but this usually is far from the truth.

nemine dissentiente
unanimously
Literally 'no one dissenting'.

Swinging final stroke

smily, and they all
that things would
of them (a polite way

Ornamented end stroke Hooks or ticks on the end denote a stubborn, intolerant nature. Acquisition can be important to the writer, especially if the hooks turn upward. As a rule, such a writer tends to be conventional on the surface but, dig a little deeper, and you may find it is just a front.

Final stroke with ornamented "hook"

End stroke that tears into paper If the end stroke tears into the paper in a downward fashion, there will be a temper with strong likes and dislikes in the person. If the stroke is made out toward the edge of the paper, it implies extravagance and generosity; just how much may be determined from the rest of the script.

acta est fabula

Final stroke tearing into paper

No end stroke By not making a final stroke, writers show that they do not always observe social niceties, and do not dwell much on the approbation of others. They are self-willed, careful about what they say or do, and may ignore or mistrust other people. As a result, they can seem rude in manner.

e, age about
ight handed.

No final stroke

3:5 **Punctuation**

USE YOUR TOOLKIT

Punctuation, or the lack of it, is a measure of a writer's attention to detail. Good punctuation in neat and tidy handwriting always has a more positive impact than poor punctuation in badly written script. Most writers tend to take care as they write, but if they become too involved with what they are trying to say, small but important details like commas or periods may be missed or ignored altogether.

Writers who dot every "i" and cross every "t" demonstrate that they are conformists, people who do what is expected. What they learned at school has simply been carried over into adulthood.

Positioning punctuation

In English, punctuation marks should be placed after or before words on the baseline unless they are meant to be above it, for example, apostrophes or quotation marks. In languages such as French or German, where accent marks are used, care must be taken to place them over or under the correct letters.

When properly positioned, such punctuation indicates its writer had a careful, measured outlook at the time of writing. However, when this small feature suddenly flies high up above the baseline, the writer is showing a more carefree spirit.

Generally speaking, most punctuation follows the end of a word, divides, or ends a sentence. It may emphasize a point being made. The freedom of expression allowed to writers at such times is most revealing and a strongly significant element in graphology.

Marks below the baseline A period or other mark placed well below the baseline signifies depression, or that the writer is tired and feeling pessimistic. The rest of the script will bear this out.

Comma placed below the baseline

Unfortunately, it has been closed off to visitors for some years, except for special events! I was lucky in being able to visit when you could still wander among

Variable punctuation Writing that is fairly consistent means good control, but punctuation made in different places or at scattered points at the end of a letter, in a way that differs from the start of it, implies a mood change. Neat, tidy punctuation at the beginning but all over the place at the end, shows the writer's initial control has faded.

Variable punctuation— also note the variations of the "i" dot positions

good understanding of hi
Yes, like you i get the s
But, left alone he work

Excessive punctuation

Excessive punctuation Too many marks imply a show-off who exaggerates or is too emphatic. This is the sign of a worrier who cannot, does not, or will not give up long after a matter has been resolved. When a period is placed immediately after the signature, irrespective of whether only the first name or the whole name has been used, it tells you that this is the writer's last word on the subject.

r Peter — As per my e-mail... -
Best wishes,

Incorrect or omitted punctuation Marks put in the wrong place or omitted in a poor standard script shows someone who can't be bothered with details. This writer will take the opposite view of those with whom he or she is talking in order to feel different from them, or perhaps just for the sake of it.

Ellipsis placed instead of a period

3:6 "i" and "t" marks

Two important marks made in handwriting are the dotted "i" and crossed "t." There is no correct or formal way taught as to their formation, and no strictures on writing them. When writers put pen to paper, they write words but stop to dot their "i"s and cross their "t"s. Some people wait until they finish a word or sentence, then stop, lift their pens, go back and make their marks, and then begin writing again. Others do it as they go, joining the "i"-dots or "t"-bars to preceding or following letters. And, of course, there are those who may not bother to dot their "i"s or cross their "t"s at all.

"i"-DOTS

The "i"-dot belongs in the upper zone and relates to the writer's intellect and imagination. How it is made and where it is placed, high or low, with or without pressure, before or after the stem, or joined to the next word or words, will indicate its writer's attention to detail, enthusiasm, and practicality.

Position of the "i"-dot reveals writer's characteristics

etching are painted on a range of traditional hand blown and modern glass to stunning effect. With the

How the "i" is written

The letter "i" is written in two parts. After the stem has been created, the dot is placed above it. The dot should be placed so that it fits in with the handwriting, in the same way the period or other punctuation marks are made. It should be noticed, but only in passing; it must not be too conspicuous.

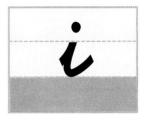

mind me writing fa a two birds with are sta and I am looking fa

"i"-dots appear here as both dots and dashes.

Appearance of the dot It may look like a small club or a dash, a wavy mark or a circle, or not be written at all. Unusual marks suggest the writer of them has special gifts. However, it is impossible to show the entire range of dots that can be made. Whole books have been written on this mark alone, and there may be as many as six or seven variations of it in any single sample of handwriting.

Wayward dots Dots that fly high show creativity and imagination, and if it looks like a small wavy line, the writer will be known for having a sense of humor. Dots that resemble clubs, or which are written as dashes, relate to irritability and bad temper. It would be unusual to see such marks made with a light stroke, unless the whole missive is written the same way, which would imply sensitivity.

Dots flying into the upper zone

Dots connected to letters Dots joined to the preceding letter indicate a cautious nature, and, to the following letter, a perceptive mind—someone always looking ahead. While this is regarded as a sign of intelligence, it also shows a lack of patience with those who dare oppose the writer.

"i"-dots connected to preceding/following letters

Circle "i"-dots

Circle "i"-dot The circle "i"-dot belongs to people who could be considered emotional misfits, those who like to be the center of attention all the time, are rather narcissistic, and are difficult to get to know well. Often they are food faddists, or try to be and appear "different." They may exhibit manual dexterity or, especially in the older writer, a degree of eccentricity.

Small "i" usage If writers write the stem of the letter "i" consistently small, they worry, lack confidence, or doubt their ability. If they use the small "i" as the personal pronoun instead of the capital letter, they will be immature, lack drive, and undervalue themselves.

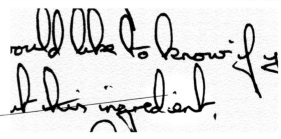

"i" smaller than other letters

"t"-BARS

The letter "t" is widely considered to be the most important letter in the Roman alphabet, a theory supported by the many publications devoted entirely to it. This may be partly because it is connected with the letter "x", used in the past as a mark of recognition. More than likely it is because of its similarity to the letter "i"—with its free stroke of the cross bar.

How the "t" is written

The way this letter is written, and how its bar is created, helps graphologists assess the level of its writer's ambition, control, discipline, drive, enthusiasm, intelligence, speed, and willpower. Again—as with the letter "i"—the letter is formed in two stages. The stem is written and the bar then placed through it. As a rule, a writer tends to do this either immediately or finishes the word and then goes back to site the bar, which should be placed so that it fits in with the rest of the script.

   A "t" should be crossed so that it is not conspicuous, as it can distract the reader and, of course, is quite evident if left out altogether. There are more than 450 distinctive ways of writing this completed letter!

Looped "t" stem A stem made with a loop at the top is a sure indication of sensitivity to criticism. This person needs constant encouragement (▶▶ **Loops**, pages 34–41).

Excessively looped "t" stems

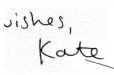

Tented "t" stem A stem that looks like a tepee reflects a closed mind with a stubborn streak. Writers who produce this will not give way, even if they realize they are wrong, but may relish being this way because it brings them recognition or attention.

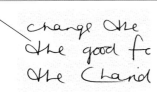

Tepee "t"

Knotted shape on the "t"

Knotted or starred "t" A variety of knotting or star shapes indicate persistence. People with these in their handwriting are tough types who have their own way of getting things done. Without the bar crossing their "t"s, this will be less prominent, but with a bar you may be certain there will be some obstinacy in their characters.

Inverted "u"/"v" stem The writer who makes a stem like an inverted letter "u" or "v" shows a slow approach to everything, someone who dislikes change of any kind, and whom nothing will change. Remember, however, that these remarks are but single factors among many. Slope, pressure, and style all must be taken into account before you make a final assessment of their meaning.

Inverted "v" stem

Types of cross-bar

Short, crossed "t" bars indicate a lack of drive and enthusiasm, and the writer of them will be reserved. A long bar suggests confidence and control, ambition, and the energy to carry out one's plans. Heavy bars indicate a determined nature, while a lightly etched bar shows someone easily influenced, shy, or retiring. A wavy bar reveals humor and a sense of fun. If a bar stems from a knot, or has one in it, the writer may have a critical nature, and will usually be persistent enough to finish what has been started.

eritas simplex oratio est

"t"-bar line a cross This often shows a superstitious nature or very personal religious convictions.

Curved cross-bars A cross-bar created from the base of the letter "t" in an upward curve to the right suggests economy with the truth. A bar made in an upward, backward curve to the left shows jealousy, lack of confidence, and unnecessary worry.

Upward-curving cross-bars

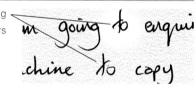

m going to enqui
chine to copy

Low-set cross-bars

find enclosed the promd
& above offer.

Low- and medium-set cross-bars A low-set "t"-bar indicates poor energy levels and limited ambition. A medium-set bar indicates average ability, while a highly set bar usually means ambition, imagination, and leadership skills.

Concave and convex cross-bars Concave "t"-bars imply repressed emotions, while convex "t"-bars reveal a willful nature but an unstable emotional response and poor self-control. When the ascending bar is like a pointing arrow, it indicates an optimist, but a descending bar shows someone with an aggressive, pessimistic, and stubborn approach. A light stroke eases this somewhat and the writer can be unrealistic. The heavy stroke shows a sense of adventure and an enjoyment of physical or outdoor activity.

Concave cross-bars

accept the respo
being a child of
to accept the be

Note the tiny ticks on the end of this convex cross-bar

want

Just a quic
re your phor

Omitted cross-bars Consistently omitted "t"-bars show an absentminded, careless nature. If the cross-bar is omitted, it shows the writer has rather strong emotions, often because of a lack of common sense. Normal handwriting will have a few missing cross-bars on the "t." This is quite normal, especially at the end of a word.

In-depth Analysis: *Job application*

A position for a salesperson within the consumer industry
was advertised and all applicants were asked to reply in
their own handwriting.

Uneven baseline shows
indecision and possibly
emotional instability

Reclined writing is an
indication of introversion.
Even the PPI leans leftward

Missing letters indicate a
lack of attention to detail

**The very formal use of
all his initials** shows
an unyielding nature

For this kind of job, the ideal candidate needs to have an extroverted and pleasant personality. The person should be able to establish a rapport with all kinds of people, possess good judgment, and be willing to travel. In addition, they also must be prepared to be away from home occasionally, sometimes for long spells, and should have a clean driver's licence.

Good salespeople must be able to express themselves well in writing. They should be persistent and have plenty of self-confidence, not to mention the determination to succeed. They may have to be part of a team whose members work together for long periods, or they may need to spend much of their day alone.

Middle zone letters with open tops suggest that this person is unable to keep a secret

Lack of upper loops confirms that this person avoids emotional issues

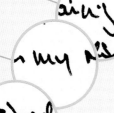

Variety of lower loops imply inner conflict

Analysis

1 From his handwriting sample, Mr. P. R. J. Thomas seems to have none of these qualities at all. His writing is reclined, always an indication of introversion and someone's reluctance to show their true feelings. Even Mr. Thomas's personal pronoun "I" (PPI) leans leftward, another sign of social reluctance.

2 His baselines are also uneven, showing indecision, someone open to the mood of the moment, opportunistic, and inclined to emotional instability. The lack of punctuation, along with a few missing letters in some of the words, shows inattention to detail.

3 Many of his middle zone letters, which should be closed off, have been made with open tops or sides, suggesting a complete inability to be trusted with confidential information. At the drop of a hat, this writer will tell all he knows.

4 There are also no properly constructed upper loops to letters that should have them. This is further confirmation that this is someone who is avoiding emotional issues. A wide variety of lower loops or tails implies inner conflict, with an attendant inability to properly direct biological urges. There is a quite a bit of inner turmoil within this man's psyche.

5 The way the signature employs each of the writer's initials shows a rather formal, unyielding nature. Mr. Thomas needs to have a set way of doing things and that means he is not very versatile and cannot think through problems quickly and efficiently. The period shows he does not like to argue or have his authority challenged. This is not the handwriting of a man you would want to represent your company.

WHAT TO LOOK FOR IN AN APPLICANT

▸ A firm and fairly even pressure in a slightly forward-slanting script = perseverance, tenacity, and leadership

▸ Examine the letters "g" and "y". When they look like an 8 and a 7 respectively = a quick mind and good judgment

▸ Equal spacing between letters; downward hooks on any "t"-bars present; a slight upward slope to the line; a legible script = an ability to work well with others

Chapter 4

The Inner Person

What are the issues preoccupying the writer's unconscious mind? Examine their signature to reveal how they wish to be viewed by others—this is our self-image on paper. Doodles, as a reflection of our inner emotional concerns, are also discussed and a gallery of possible doodles and their analyses is included.

4:1 **Signatures**

Signatures show how writers prefer to be seen and reflect the outer image they wish to project to others. The body of a letter shows the emotional, mental, and physical state of the writer. When asked to assess a single signature without a sample of any other writing, you should exercise caution, as there will be significant differences in the way a letter is signed and the way its text is written.

GRAPHOMANIA

People often use two or more different signatures. Businesspeople will create one for their professional image but retain something different for their private and personal affairs. In our early days, most of us will have practiced writing our name for the sheer pleasure of seeing it on paper. We will have experimented by copying the names of family members and other people around us.

This early form of graphomania is usually carried into adult life and is often seen in doodles. This is your persona on paper and says as much to a graphologist. Apart from being your name, it will also yield a whole wealth of information because your signature represents you, the writer.

Position in relation to the text

The further away a signature is written from the last line of text, the less its author wants to be associated with what has been written above it—and may indicate that what has been said may not be wholly truthful either. A signature placed very close to the last line of the main body of text shows the writer believes in and is honest about what is written. This is especially so if the letter is personal.

Signature placed at a distance from the body of text

Signature placed close to the body of text

Position on the page

Left of center Unless taught to place their signatures to the right, most people sign their letters slightly to the left of center, which is relatively normal. This indicates caution with a hint of a self-defense or self-protection.

Fred Bloggs

Extreme left When the signature appears at the extreme left of a page, there will be a lack of confidence and slight reserve in the writer. If this is in keeping with the policy of the company where the individual works, though, you cannot analyze the signature in this manner. It would be wise to find out about this before moving on, because if this is the case, it suggests the writer does not have enough initiative to become free of the work-place influence.

Jill Jones

Center Writers who place their signatures precisely in the center of a page like to be at the forefront of things as much as possible. However, they will display an element of caution or bluff that only those close to them will notice.

John Doe

Right of center A signature placed slightly to the right of center, and at a reasonable distance from the last line, shows the writer to have initiative and a relatively outgoing and sociable nature.

Jane Smith

Extreme right A signature at the extreme right of a page shows its writer has a lively, active personality. However, some impatience with the "system" may be present because this person does not take too kindly to petty bureaucracy.

Pete Johnson

Forged signatures

Society and the law recognize signatures as being unique and an act of forgery incurs a heavy penalty. This is most important, for it acknowledges that your signature reflects your own character and personality, and nowhere in graphology is this emphasized more. Often, this is where an expert in fraud will start an investigation, because it is so often the most difficult part of our writing to forge.

Size of signature

Well-balanced with the text A clear, easily understood, and well-balanced signature without embellishment indicates a reliable, steady, but fairly conservative character.

Signature legible and same size as main body of text

Smaller than the main body of text This suggests introversion. The writer is sensitive and mild, but may also be a schemer who sets out to deliberately give such an impression in order to gain some kind of advantage.

A small script with an even smaller signature

Larger than the text This shows a confident, determined, and forceful character who moves smoothly through life and is brought down by very little.

Signature slightly larger than main body

Considerably larger than the text A writer whose signature is quite considerably larger than the above-written text shows its author is selfish and has an over-bearing outlook. This is someone not very nice to know, who comes across as over-confident, proud, and even pretentious.

A very prominent signature

Size of capitals

Over-emphasized capitals

If any of the capital letters in a signature are over-emphasized, its author will have materialistic leanings. Such a writer desires position and status either at work or socially, and will be prepared to do virtually anything to attain this.

Both capitals here are over-emphasised

Small capital letters

A signature with small capital letters shows its writer has a tendency to undervalue personal abilities and other skills. This is the sign of the drifter.

A very small capital begins this signature

Above-average-height capital letters This suggests self-obsession, and someone who will use others for their own ends.

A very large capital "T"

Same size as the rest of the signature This suggests someone with poor ambition and a reasonably modest nature.

Capital same size as rest of signature

Assessing style

Whenever possible, try to work on more than one example of a signature. For instance, a signature made when a writer is in good health will be different to one made when unwell. A small point, perhaps, but the signature of someone who has changed their surname can be easily misinterpreted if they have not yet decided how to sign the new name. In this period of adjustment, the forename may appear slightly larger than the new surname. No two signatures are written the same way any more than there are two sets of identical finger prints and, while a signature tends to stay the same for a long time if the writer is disturbed in any way, it can and does vary.

Analysis In a proper analysis, a few lines of text in the writer's usual style should be compared with the signature. It is even more helpful to have several signatures, and samples written at different times, because handwriting can and does vary so much.

Emphasized but legible The large, emphasized, or exaggerated signature implies a healthy ego, but one which may have some some inferiority problems. Look at the rest of the handwriting for further evidence to support this.

Legible—and placed to right of center and close to last lines

Emphasized and illegible An illegible signature that cannot be deciphered or read properly is an example of bad manners, rudeness, and thoughtlessness on the part of the writer, who cares only for what has been written and not for his or her readers.

Large—emphasized, encircled, underlined, and exaggerated

Full name signed

Name signed in full Writers who sign their first- and middle-names and surname in full display a sense of self-importance.

Final punctuation A period placed after a signature is a writer's way of telling you that this is the last word on the subject and the matter is now closed. A colon, or even a semi-colon, found here suggests the writer might entertain more discussion, but is really quite reluctant to pursue the subject any further at the time of writing.

Underlined and periods

Underlining The flourish or paraph was originally created to offset the possibility of forgery. People who underline their signatures may be cautious and use the line as a prop to help support their ideas in much the same vein as the lead-in stroke (▶ *Lead-in strokes*, page 56). Some graphologists are of the opinion that underlining suggests self-confidence. In most cases, this is quite true, but such apparent confidence can come from an element of doubt.

The heavy paraph shows energy and enthusiasm, but there may be a sense of limitation in such writers, who will not allow anyone very close until they can be certain of their motives. This kind of writer is unlikely to permit the use of first names in business matters and this signature will probably be found most often in the commercial world.

Underlined signature

Overscoring An overscore created over the top of a signature is not often seen. This implies a stern insistence upon self-protection. The writer will be selfish and dislike change.

When an over- and underscore appear above and below a signature, expect to find someone who is quite unable to trust others, even those who think they are close to the person. This is a sign of a lonely, reserved character who is always suspicious of the motives of others.

Over- and underscored signature—also note period

Double paraph The double paraph made below signatures means their writers have determination, a strong desire for personal recognition, and a need for status either at work or socially. These writers feel they deserve this, and are convinced of their talents. Unfortunately, if such talents are present, they may not always be used wisely by people of this type. This is another sign of selfishness.

The weight of the stroke shows a 2-line paraph

Curlicues and flourishes
Elaborate curlicues, exotic designs, and flourishes may reflect ostentation and an inflated ego.

An elaborate, over-worked capital "E"

Short underline Occasionally, a short line may be written under just a first-name. This is an indication of informality. When found under the surname only, the writer prefers a formal approach until deciding otherwise. A first-name with several syllables and a short paraph under the last one shows the writer dislikes the name being abbreviated (preferring Peter, not Pete, for example). Someone who may be unable to mix well with others is revealed if the paraph strikes through the name or a part of it. Such a person may appear deceptive or shallow.

A short underline beneath the surname only

The "X"-formation

If you see an "X"-formation, or a series of "X"s within a signature (like an unfinished loop), its author is likely to be emotionally disturbed for a number of reasons. A recent bereavement or a long-term partnership, emotional or commercial, may have come to an end for the person. Something somewhere has become too much for the writer, who is showing signs of beginning to buckle or giving way under the strain.

This "X"-formation almost always seems like an "airbrush" stroke, where the pen begins a mark—usually a loop—but with insufficient pressure to maintain it all the way through. It is a symbol of a quite serious loss of self-esteem.

A good example of an "X"-formation in a signature

In-depth Analysis: *Postcard home*

Perhaps it is when we are on vacation, have few apparent cares, and are well rested that we should be able to sit down and write those postcards that everyone has asked to receive. This is in line with the popular notion that, if nothing else, all is well while we are vacationing, and that, when we write, we will use our natural script. Probably this will be true, unless something goes wrong.

The four-and-a-half lines on this postcard from the author's friend Jo were not written in her usual style. On examining how she had penned her message, it was clear that she had had an experience that had upset her. It was impossible to tell what exactly, only that something had occurred, for this was not Jo's ordinary handwriting.

Generally she claims to be comfortable being one of the crowd and enjoys ordinary social intercourse, but her handwriting here is saying the absolute opposite. She seems to be uneasy with people who she imagines may make demands upon her or who are too "clinging" in approach. She has opted to be more isolated. The fewer the people who are allowed to share her personal sphere, the better, as far as she is concerned. Instead of being one of the girls as usual, her writing is conveying her feeling that she wants to be an onlooker or observer. At the time of writing, she does not feel she wants to take an active part in social activities.

The last line sums it all up. She needs a shoulder to cry on and is silently asking for the author's.

IS SOMEONE REALLY HAPPY? LOOK FOR:

▸ Rounded loops in the upper or lower zones

▸ Garland connections

▸ Steady or regular rhythm within the script

▸ Defined extensions on the end strokes — but not too long.

Omission of the "r" denotes forgetfulness, brought on by anxiety

Difference in letter sizes shows that the writer is not thinking clearly and objectively

Analysis

1 She does not complete the opening word: "Dear," omitting the letter "r." An omission in such a simple word implies forgetfulness brought on by emotional anxiety and tension.

2 She also fails to create a good capital "P" for "Peter," and the spacing between all of the words and lines does not at all reflect her normally very companionable nature. The small letter "p" for "Peter" could indicate how she may be feeling about men—or at least one man. This is a classic sign of someone who has just had an argument. It indicates that Jo has probably had a quarrel with her boyfriend, as she is emotionally off-balance.

3 Jo normally spaces her words and lines much more closely together than she has here. This, and the wide spaces between words and lines, indicate that she has chosen to isolate herself emotionally and interpersonally. She does not like the idea of other people being too close to her and does not want to be touched or held.

4 Something is interfering with her objective thinking, which is shown by the more-than-excessive spacing she has used, together with the differences in letter sizes in the third line. This suggests that things have gotten a little out of hand and that she cannot correlate or integrate her thoughts properly. She has lost sight of the big picture.

Using a lower-case where a capital should be, as in the small "p" here, is the classic sign of someone who has just had an argument

Excessive word spacing suggests emotional isolation

NIAGARA FALLS: In operation since 1846, the Maid of the ... of the most exciting ways to view Niagara Falls. Raingear... cruise to the base of the Falls.

Reflections of Niagara

peter,

true

is very

Dear Peter,

I'm having a lovely time
The food is very good,
the people are very nice.
night life is fantastic. Wish
be here as well.

NIAGARA F

4:2 **Doodles**

Doodles are created in an unconscious fashion by people whose minds are totally absorbed elsewhere; the doodle is a graphic expression of the unconscious state. It is said that a picture paints a thousand words, so the analysis of doodles has become a natural extension of graphological assessment.

UNDERSTANDING DOODLES

People doodle because it helps ease anxiety and relieve tension. It is now widely accepted that a doodle is a physical projection of a writer's inner emotional desires. This is considered so much the case that any drawings made when people take part in pre-promotion or new-job activities are likely to be collected in and analyzed by potential employers, along with their handwriting.

Irrespective of the cause, which may be emotional, psychological, sexual, or social, we are most likely to doodle when unable to proceed with a task, as, for instance, when waiting for someone, or for something to happen. These little drawings are often created while we are on the phone, and we make them anywhere and everywhere—on whatever scraps of paper we may have on hand at the time.

A doodle is not handwriting, but a collection of scribbles of blobs, dots, lines, and squiggles made over and over again repetitively. People tend to re-create the same patterns or designs while their minds are exercised elsewhere. There are some people who do not make these little pictures at all; they are said to be well-controlled, direct, precise, and straight to the point in their manner at all times.

Position

Left of page A doodle drawn on the left-hand side of a page implies inner reserve, someone cautious where others are concerned, for this doodler does not make new friends readily. Past incidents and people mean a lot to this person, who has trouble trying to forget. Strictly speaking, the person is not unresponsive, but just unable to freely display emotions publicly.

Right of page A doodle on the right of a page shows a more outgoing and socially orientated character. The future attracts this doodler, who looks forward to it and is ready for tomorrow. This progressive person enjoys others' company and needs to be with people; the past holds very little attraction.

Center of page A centrally placed doodle implies an extrovert, someone who needs to be noticed and makes sure that others do not forget their presence.

Upper page A doodle drawn toward the top of a page implies an idealistic, optimistic character who needs to keep both feet on the ground without getting too carried away with a constant flow of ideas.

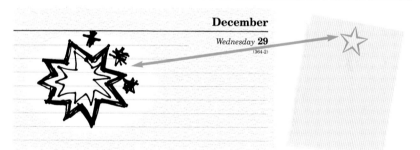

Lower page A drawing set lower suggests someone with a less extroverted nature. No matter how gifted the person might be, a reluctance to self-promote marks this writer.

A repeated design suggests emotional or mental compulsion. It is not the time for hard decision-making, for the mood of the moment rules.

Pressure

Heavy pressure Writers who exhibit obvious heavy pressure when drawing doodles indicate that they are responding very much to their interpretations of their moods of the moment. An element of stress with a degree of aggression or an outright display of temper may accompany these doodles in some cases.

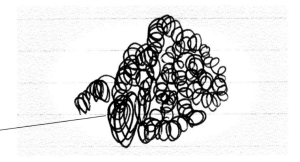

Heavy pressure
implies some stress

Medium pressure This implies a fairly balanced and reasonable mood. So the subject matter of these doodles will probably be a lead to any discrepancy in the writer's normal behavior.

A balanced mood is
seen in a medium
pressure

Light pressure This shows a receptive and sensitive type, someone liable to being easily influenced.

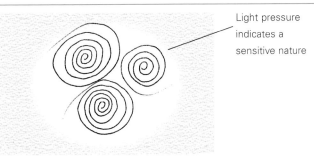

Light pressure
indicates a
sensitive nature

Variable pressure Pressure that shows obvious differences symbolizes instability, someone up one moment and down the next. For as long as the pressure varies like this, the doodler will be unreliable.

Variations in pressure here
demonstrate instability

Shading Shaded drawings imply anxiety, founded or unfounded; their authors may have talked themselves into negative thinking patterns and are unable to trace a clear path out of their problem(s).

Shading and cross-hatching suggest a negative attitude

Curved/straight lines Curved and wavy lines imply an emotional reaction to what the doodler thinks is going on. Remember, a doodle is someone's unconscious reaction to their interpretation of a situation. Straight lines are more constructive and can betray a measure of aggression and determination.

A combination of curved and straight lines indicates emotional defensiveness and/or aggression

Underlining Emotional defensiveness is also suggested when writers underline everything, as if to create a platform on which to stand in order to stop sinking further. If a paraph is placed at the top of this sketch, read it as a sign of protection from those in authority.

An underline may also show defensiveness

Color, shading, and lines

Doodles are sometimes created in color or several colors and may be drawn almost anywhere at any time. As a rule, doodlers tend to draw in the same color as their normal pen. Some people, however, like to use different colors as they doodle. As with all graphological assessments, you should not pronounce on the strength of one, two, or even more doodles. A doodle is a definite reflection of the mood of the moment, so if an analysis is made some days or weeks later, the problems reflected in the drawing(s) might already have been resolved.

Pink reveals a feminine side in both men and women.

Blue indicates reflection.

Red is a stimulant and reflects energy and sexuality.

Brown almost always suggests a problem with personal security and common sense.

Green may imply a degree of envy or jealousy was present when the doodle was drawn.

Yellow tends to be a reflection of financial worries and/or material matters, although when found in a healing environment, there may be a health inference involved.

Gray is a sign of an impartial nature, a neutral observer in the middle of everyone else's troubles. This color often symbolizes depression or defeat.

Purple, violet, or lilac shades are a sign of a need for emotional consistency. As a rule, when any of these colors are used, the doodler is feeling extremely sensitive emotionally. A woman who uses this color will be a very feminine soul while a man is likely to have a very artistic, creative, and gentle nature.

Black is used by anxious, irritable, and tense people, and may be seen just before they launch a last attempt to restore the status quo. It is always a sign of a writer wanting to be clearly understood.

THE MEANING OF COMMON DOODLES

The study of doodles stems from the researches of Freud and Jung, and has helped to create "analytical drawing psychology" whereby an analyst is able to define an author's feelings by studying what he or she has drawn while their mind has been occupied elsewhere. The following common doodles are grouped to demonstrate four important human preoccupations: aspirations, sexuality and the body, emotions, and frustrations.

Aspirations

Arrows Arrows or ascending straight lines show ambition and aspirations. Arrows used as part of a design imply an element of calculation within the doodler. When the arrows or lines point downward, the negative side of things presently occupy the person's mind. A small series of lines close together suggest a blunt, no-nonsense type.

Upward-pointing arrows indicate an ambitious nature

Ladders A ladder suggests a social climber. The position of anything, or any person, drawn on one of the rungs, could represent the doodler, how far (up the ladder) they have come, or have yet to go.

A series of ladders demonstrates social climbing

Stars show a determination to succeed

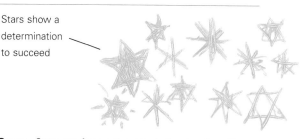

Stars Stars are frequent subjects for doodlers. They signify an ambitious nature, someone who will succeed and may well bend a few rules to be sure of achieving aims. Stars signify a very determined and aggressive person, whose ideas, however, may be all in the mind. Note the color used or writing style for further clues.

Patterns Symmetrical patterns suggest an organizer. The more complex the doodle, the better the executive power. When shading of any kind is included, the writer's drive may be lacking.

A complex pattern suggests organizational abilities and power

Money Most of the time, a doodle involving money is a sure sign that the doodler wants more of it, or the benefits it brings: comfort, ease, and security. Doodles of money, their symbols ($, £, etc.), signs, or coins, imply a degree of greed or selfishness in other ways. The writer may be unsympathetic to the wants and needs of others.

Piles of money show a craving for material comforts

Music Musical notes are rarely made by those who have little interest in music. They suggest that the writer has creative talents directed toward the arts. An excess of such symbols could also mean a sense of humor.

Musical notes indicate a leaning toward the arts

Books Books that are drawn open show a healthy interest in furthering knowledge. Closed books also show a desire to know more, but imply in addition that the doodler can keep a secret. A series of books implies method and order, and, possibly, something of a show-off.

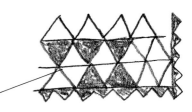

Desire for knowledge is symbolized by books

Triangles Triangles imply aggression, ambition, and energy. For many people, it is also a sexual symbol. Someone who doodles triangles has a constructive mind, with a good level of perception, and knows how to deal with people, enjoying solving problems, also being quite prepared to sacrifice anything (or anyone, at times) to achieve personal aims.

Triangles demonstrate ambition, and problem-solving abilities

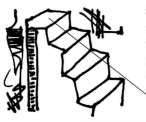

Steps Steps are a sign of an ambitious nature, and possibly sexual problems. If the steps rise to a dead end, it means that the doodler's plans may not succeed and that they may have to be re-thought. If a series of steps are drawn side-by-side and fill a page from side-to-side, the doodler is a fairly flexible type, someone who is not discouraged by failure, and is always ready to try again.

Steps also show ambition, yet these rise to a dead end suggesting fear of failure

Houses House doodles symbolize safety and security. The more detailed the drawing, the more the doodler is an idealist. If a garden is included, then a very short path to the door indicates a more settled nature, while a long path shows a guarded one.

A longing for security is seen in a house doodle

Wheels When wheels are properly drawn so that they are quite different from an ordinary circle, the doodle shows mental alertness. If the wheels are depicted as rolling forward, they indicate independence. Wheels shown rolling backward suggest the writer is overly concerned with past glories.

A wheel shows mental alertness

Sexuality and the body

Eyes How the eye is drawn is significant because it may mean anything from selfishness and self-absorption to sexual problems. Female eyes with long lashes suggest a flirtatious nature and, if heavy eyebrows are also drawn, there is a sexual connotation. The eyes are the mirror of the soul. Once again, the drawing might give some additional clues.

Long lashes demonstrate a flirtatious nature

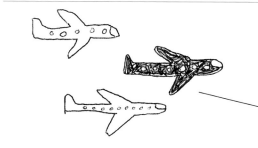

Airplanes Airplanes are basically phallic symbols. An airliner suggests the writer wants to get away. There may be a holiday looming or it may have just finished. A warplane is an indication of violence. A helicopter infers indecision.

Airplanes, and other phallic symbols, suggest a preoccupation with sex

Snakes Snakes are a sign of wisdom and sexual prowess. If coiled snakes are drawn, it shows a certain amount of rebellion and a stubborn attitude. A snake at rest, long and flexible, shows the writer is more open to suggestion.

Snakes symbolize sexual prowess

Body parts When body parts are continually drawn, it shows an interest in that part of the body at the time. In older people, this may be related to a health matter. In the young, it may be sexual; adolescent boys may draw breasts, while young girls draw the penis or phallic symbols.

Body parts imply a concern with that part of the body

Emotions

Hearts Hearts are a sign of emotional vulnerability very near the surface and often appear in a doodler's repertoire after a relationship has broken up. The more heart shapes there are, the more emotional the writer. If hearts are drawn one inside the other, it is a sign of a need for more affection to be given or received.

A large group of hearts implies a very emotional writer

Faces When a face is drawn in profile, it can mean a recent or current relationship difficulty. Happy faces mean all is well, but sad or serious faces imply a lack of cooperation with or by others is the root of the difficulty. This is a person who dislikes being subjected to the caprices of others. When a hat covers the head, or one eye, of the doodled face, the author is showing a self-protective streak. Self-portraiture is always an extension of the ego, whether it is complimentary or not.

A hat on the head shows self-protection

Names To doodle your own name suggests a strong ego because you think a lot about yourself. If one of the names you doodle is encircled, there may be some extra worry concerning someone you know with that name. Youngsters often enjoy doodling their own names or signatures. It is always worth comparing the person's ordinary signature with the doodled version.

Lovers will often doodle each other's names

Animals Drawing animals implies a fondness for them in general. The doodler may want one for a pet, or the nature associated with the animal might refer to the problem or his personality. Thus, an elephant may mean a weight problem; a lion, leadership; a monkey or a parrot, a sense of humor.

Doodled caricature of a dog

Boxes Boxes indicate a controlled and controlling nature. The writer is precise, logical, and practical. When any of the boxes have been shaded in, not unlike a chess board, the doodler will show extra attention to detail. Shading admits a more emotional approach.

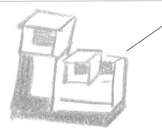

Shaded boxes indicate control and attention to detail

Frames show a need to feel secure

Anticipation is suggested by a spring

Frames Frames or borders placed around a doodle act like a fence and suggests the writer is torn between a desire for more freedom but has an inner wish for more basic protection and security. A fence can have holes, but frames and borders do not.

Spirals/springs Spirals are usually created from small or large circular formats. When expanded from the smaller version, as in a spring, their writer is full of tension, as if expecting the unexpected but ready to meet the challenge. Spirals are symbolic of expansion and optimism. If intertwined or decreasing in size, things may be too much for the doodler, suggesting depression or a negative outlook.

Trees An American lecturer in psychology devised a special test many years ago involving trees. He discovered over 25 ways to sketch or doodle a tree and through his analyses reached a very high degree of accuracy in his findings.

The type of tree drawn represents someone's inner nature. If leaves or branches point upward, an optimistic person is indicated. When drawn pointing downward, the writer may be depressed. A well-rounded tree shows a pleasant sociable nature; pointed or hard-angled versions suggest a touchy personality. If ground is drawn around the base, it can mean anxiety, reservation, or unrealistic thinking.

Rounded trees indicate sociability

Birds Birds suggest the desire to fly away and leave it all behind. Big birds, or birds of prey, imply feelings of resentment. A doodler of this type can wait a long time to get even, revenge being best eaten cold in this person's mind.

Birds signify a desire to get away

Sentimentality is seen in doodles of flowers

Flowers All flower drawings have an emotionally orientated preoccupation associated with them. The flower itself may denote how much this is so; it helps to have some knowledge of the language of flowers. The flower doodler may be a sentimentalist. Heavy pressure may carry some sexual meaning. Light pressure shows a desire for a return to what a relationship used to mean.

Waves Should waves be predominantly garlanded, the drawing suggests an open and friendly nature. Arcade waves are an indication of a secretive nature, someone who knows how to cover their tracks. Anything shown in the water—whether things or people—may represent the source of a problem in subconcious contemplation. If these items are drawn underwater, the doodler cannot yet see any real answer to the worry at the time the doodle is being made.

Arcade waves suggest a secretive nature

Frustrations

Someone frustrated by circumstances may doodle lucky symbols

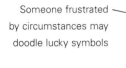 

Lucky charms A doodle that illustrates any symbol of luck, like a four-leaf clover, a horseshoe, or the number 7, suggests the writer feels cheated. In some ways, it is a cry for help, for the doodler feels it is about time their luck changed for the better, without extra effort from him or her.

Figures Doodling with numbers suggests money problems, unless the same figure is constantly repeated within the pattern. If the same number is doodled repeatedly, it might indicate the number of people or things preventing a problem being solved.

The figure "1" is often written as a substitute for the personal pronoun "I" (PPI). The PPI represents the ego. Too many number ones in a doodle can imply egocentricity.

Repetition of a figure suggests this is the number of people/things causing a problem

Mazes A doodle involving a maze or a web-like pattern suggests inner conflict. There may be frustration at a lack of achievement and the author may be confused as to what the next step should be. The doodler's mind will continue to work toward a satisfactory result.

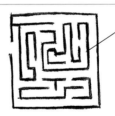

Mazes also indicate frustration

Boats Like birds, boats represent a desire to get away from it all. However, a large ocean liner shows a love of and desire for luxury. Speedboats suggest an adventurous nature. Sailboats indicate a dreamer.

As with warplanes, warboats demonstrate aggression

Dots Drawings made with lots of dots show the doodler has the ability to concentrate. If linked by lines, the writer may be frustrated, unable to bring a project or other aim to fruition. Such a picture is often symbolic in these cases.

Here, dots, and dots linked by lines, suggest high levels of concentration, but also frustration

Shaded clouds indicate some emotional conflict

Clouds Small, unshaded, fluffy clouds denote escapism. If filled in, the writer has difficulty when dealing with his or her emotional and sexual problems. A whole series of clouds of all shapes or sizes indicates a well-disposed personality. If rain is shown falling from them, the author may spend a lot of time trying to cross bridges before getting to them.

Circles All completed circles are a symbol of independence. Incomplete circles suggest a more flexible approach. The doodler may well cooperate, but only up to a point. Drawing circles is also a sign of a lazy streak. The author of any circular doodle tends to be a dreamer. Rows and rows of circles show a desire to solve problems without too much hassle. Circles can also refer to a sexual problem. There is very little aggression in the author of circles.

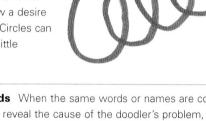

Completed circles show a need or wish for independence

Words When the same words or names are constantly repeated, they often reveal the cause of the doodler's problem, especially if the words are discernible. Use basic graphology techniques to compare the doodled words with their author's handwritten version of them.

This doodler is possibly an over-achiever

Fences imply a desire for protection from some anxiety

Fences Fences are meant to keep things in, or out. Whenever a fence appears, whatever it surrounds is the probable cause of the worry. If it is a name, then the person with that name is not being very helpful.

Squares As a rule, squares indicate aggression and constructive ability. Whether interlocked, side by side, or one on top of another, the writer does not take kindly to opposition and likes an ordered life. Squares drawn within squares suggest frustration. The doodler is unable to resolve current difficulties.

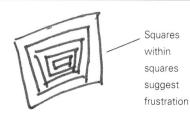

Squares within squares suggest frustration

A narrow left-hand margin
could indicate that this person
is trying to forget the past ④

In-depth Analysis: *Love cheat?*

Janice and Mark were found together at a time and place that suggested a
potential tryst, and Mike, Janice's husband, accused her of infidelity. They
have been unable to talk it over sensibly, so Janice has written to Mike.

Disconnected letters ⑤
always imply a restless,
impatient, and selfish nature

Analysis

1 The overall presentation of the
letter is messy and untidy. The
tangling of the upper and lower
extensions, in some cases involving
the middle zone as well, suggests
emotional confusion at the time
of writing.

2 Every line contains a variety of
letter sizes in the middle zone. This
shows that Janice was extremely
upset when she put pen to paper.
As graphologists, we must ask

**HOW CAN YOU TELL IF
SOMEONE IS SINCERE?
LOOK FOR:**

▸ Closed tops to "a" and
"o" letters

▸ A fairly fast speed with a
distinct slant to the right

▸ An even baseline

▸ Signature should be the
same size as the rest of
the missive.

---

whether she acts like this normally,
or has the whole episode thrown
her off-balance? The variously sized
loops of the "d" and "t" indicate a
nature that is highly sensitive to any
form of criticism.

3 Each time the same two letters
appear beside each other within a
word in this letter, neither is written
in the same manner. Look at line
2's "happened," line 9's "chatting,"
line 10's "between," line 11's
"good," line 12's "meet," and line
14's "all." When doubles of the
letters "l" and "p" are different, a
writer tends to be unpredictable or
inconsistent, and will exhibit a lack
of physical control. Much the same
may be inferred from a double letter
"t." Two letter "e"s often appear
different, but when double "o"s are
not the same, writers are informing
others that they are protecting their
own interests, and that not
everything they say or do (or write!)
should be taken at face value.

4 The letter's narrow left-hand
margin suggests the past holds
little attraction for Janice. However,
she needs to be accepted socially
despite her occasional displays of
over-familiarity or tactlessness.

5 Overall, this script seems cursive
but, upon closer examination, one
can see that it contains a lot of
disconnected letters. This always
implies a restless nature,
impatience, moodiness, and
selfishness. The individual responds
to the mood of the moment and
does not stop to consider the
outcome of a proposed action. The
use of an ampersand (&) that looks
like a looped letter "x" on its side
shows an agile mind.

6 Janice's letter contains
inconsistent word spacing, and
there are quite a few wide spaces
within her narrowly spaced lines.
This shows a desire for affection
along with a need to be accepted,
but that she does not always
show it.

7 Janice's signature is composed
with a clearly defined triangle
instead of a loop at the bottom of
the letter "J." As a rule, a
downward-pointing triangle in a
woman's script shows someone
who enjoys experiencing things
emotionally and physically, and may
be aggressive. Quite often, it is also
a sign of someone who is difficult
to live with.

Entangled upper and lower extensions suggest emotional confusion

1

many hur...
to Explain

2

that *what*

Varying size "d" and "t" loops indicate someone who is sensitive to criticism

2

ndde
Nened

The same two letters appearing together in a word can show an inconsistent or unpredictable nature if they are different

3

happened
do loe
between
god fre

The change of slant in this line, which should be a statement of truth, is an indication of lying

---

Mike

You said many hurtful things & every time I
tried to explain what actually happened
I wasn't able to do so. I do love
you very much & was not doing anything
with Mark that made you go off the
way you did.
He is a dear friend & we have known
each other a long time. We often spend
a lot of time together just chatting.
There is nothing between us at all
We are very good friends & that
is all
Please tell me where we can meet &
talk this one like adults.

All my love
Janie

5

&

An ampersand like a looped "x" on its side is the sign of an agile mind

6

...y time.
...e together ju...
...thing between
...d good fre

Inconsistent word spacing shows a desire for affection

7

Ja...

A downward pointing triangle is quite often a sign of someone who is difficult to live with

Chapter 5

The Graphologist's Alphabet

This graphologist's alphabet analyzes various formations of lower case letters. This is where we observe core character and personality traits such as self-confidence and emotional responsiveness. In addition, a numerical lexicon demonstrates that the way we create numbers is a significant outward expression of our inner material concerns.

The letter *a*

USE YOUR TOOLKIT

The first letter of the alphabet is "a." In most handwriting, "a" letters tend to vary in their appearance. Some will be closed and some open, while others may be narrow or wide. This is quite normal, although a consistent version shows a tendency toward the indicated trait. If all the letters are closed but fairly broad, the writer's nature is reasonably honest, fair, and broadminded.

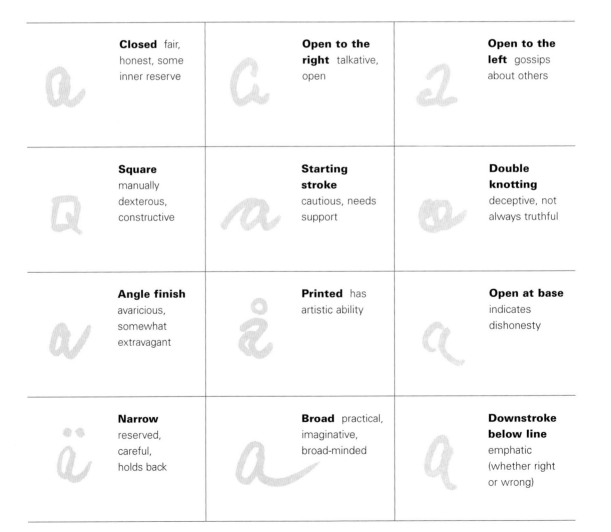

Closed fair, honest, some inner reserve	**Open to the right** talkative, open	**Open to the left** gossips about others
Square manually dexterous, constructive	**Starting stroke** cautious, needs support	**Double knotting** deceptive, not always truthful
Angle finish avaricious, somewhat extravagant	**Printed** has artistic ability	**Open at base** indicates dishonesty
Narrow reserved, careful, holds back	**Broad** practical, imaginative, broad-minded	**Downstroke below line** emphatic (whether right or wrong)

The letter *b*

A well-written "b" shows a contented nature. Whenever two letter "b"s are written together, they should look the same. Where they are not, there is a lack of confidence and poor self-control with, perhaps, a touch of instability in the writer's overall makeup.

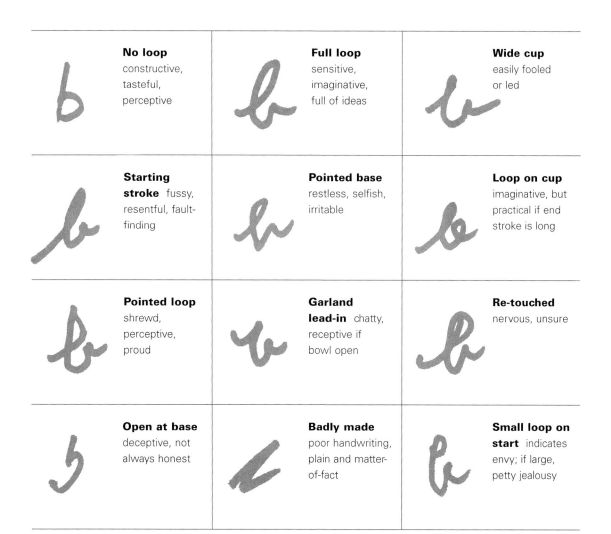

No loop
constructive, tasteful, perceptive

Full loop
sensitive, imaginative, full of ideas

Wide cup
easily fooled or led

Starting stroke fussy, resentful, fault-finding

Pointed base
restless, selfish, irritable

Loop on cup
imaginative, but practical if end stroke is long

Pointed loop
shrewd, perceptive, proud

Garland lead-in chatty, receptive if bowl open

Re-touched
nervous, unsure

Open at base
deceptive, not always honest

Badly made
poor handwriting, plain and matter-of-fact

Small loop on start indicates envy; if large, petty jealousy

The letter *c*

This letter is associated with new ideas, beliefs, and interests. When written without a starting stroke the writer can assimilate new data quite easily and he or she will be relatively self-sufficient. If there is a lead-in stroke, the past may hold more than just a passing interest. Two consecutive letter "c"s should appear consistent suggesting good mental control.

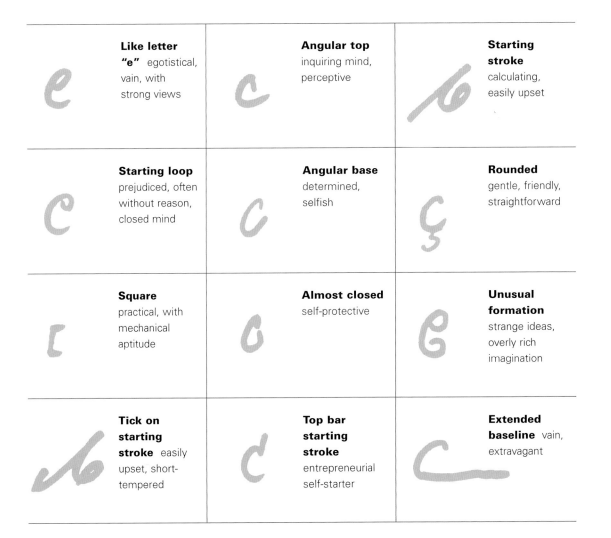

Like letter "e" egotistical, vain, with strong views	**Angular top** inquiring mind, perceptive	**Starting stroke** calculating, easily upset
Starting loop prejudiced, often without reason, closed mind	**Angular base** determined, selfish	**Rounded** gentle, friendly, straightforward
Square practical, with mechanical aptitude	**Almost closed** self-protective	**Unusual formation** strange ideas, overly rich imagination
Tick on starting stroke easily upset, short-tempered	**Top bar starting stroke** entrepreneurial self-starter	**Extended baseline** vain, extravagant

The letter *d*

The "d" reveals social aspirations and abilities, and, if poorly made, can indicate the writer's temperament of the moment. Two "d" letters together that are formed the same way show a consistent approach. High levels of obstinacy and sensitivity may also be indicated from the formation of the letter "d".

Steepled formation
stubborn, obstinate, awkward

Tall, wide loop sensitive to criticism, touchy, vulnerable

Greek form
loves culture, mature, perceptive

Short stem
independent, modest, has poor social adaptability

Tall stem
ambitious, practical, idealistic

Reversed
difficult, rebellious, "different"

Open top
talkative, cannot keep secrets, untrustworthy

Pot lid willful, likes own way, stubborn

Square loop
aggressive, dexterous, likes things simple

Open base
dishonest, dislikes responsibility

Stem curves forward
pleasure-loving, flirtatious

Broken stem
touchy, hypersensitive, someone with unstable moods

The letter *e*

The letter "e" often ends a word or a sentence and, as such, takes on added importance, especially when it occurs as the last letter in a line. Look to this letter for indications of self-protection, a brusque tongue, humor, and shrewdness.

Two letter "e"s written together in exactly the same manner will show a steady approach, but if widely different, there will be some inner instability in the writer at the time of writing.

Wide nosy, talkative, socially gregarious	**Angular base** calculating, irritable, indicates a temper	**Small "eye"** ambitious, optimistic, wishful
Long end stroke warm, sensitive, considerate	**Curled end stroke** self-protective, introverted, cautious	**Greek form** good manners, hesitant, with cultural interests
Long center bar flexible, indulgent, voluble	**Ends below baseline** reserved, easily turned off, indicates a temper	**Flat and long end stroke** cautious, inquisitive, suspicious
Heavy end stroke someone physical, inconsiderate, with a temper	**Garland end stroke** open, friendly, easy to get along with	**Like letters** selfish, vain, with a cruel streak

The letter

A well-balanced letter "f" signifies an inwardly contented writer, so two together will reveal just how deep that contentment is. Exaggeration in any of the three zones suggests a failure in that area. This letter is very much associated with the physical approach to the author's everyday social talents and, in some cases, his or her sex life.

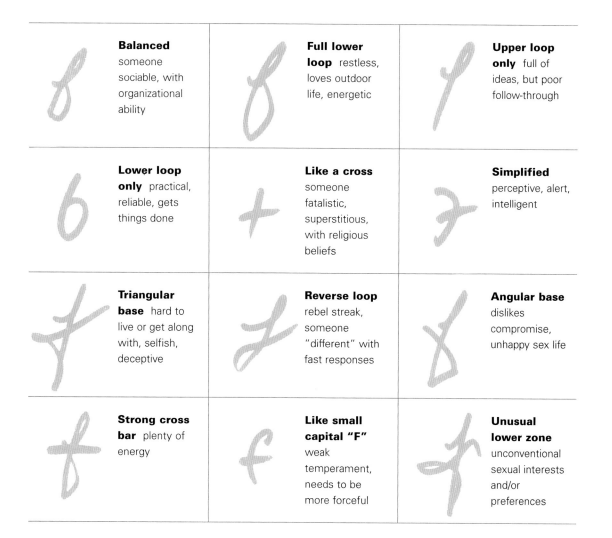

Balanced someone sociable, with organizational ability

Full lower loop restless, loves outdoor life, energetic

Upper loop only full of ideas, but poor follow-through

Lower loop only practical, reliable, gets things done

Like a cross someone fatalistic, superstitious, with religious beliefs

Simplified perceptive, alert, intelligent

Triangular base hard to live or get along with, selfish, deceptive

Reverse loop rebel streak, someone "different" with fast responses

Angular base dislikes compromise, unhappy sex life

Strong cross bar plenty of energy

Like small capital "F" weak temperament, needs to be more forceful

Unusual lower zone unconventional sexual interests and/or preferences

The letter g

How the letter "g" is written reflects people's attitudes to material possessions, and their drive, physical energy, and libido. A variety of tails implies low physical self-control, perhaps even anger with themselves when things do not work out properly. In a low standard script, different lower case formations can refer to poor coordination.

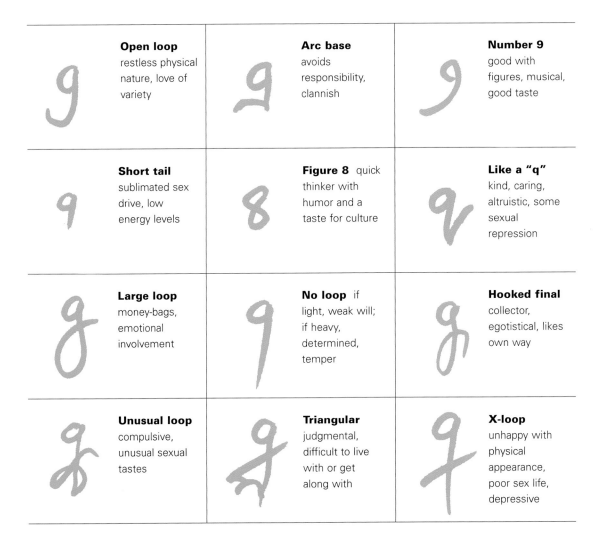

Open loop restless physical nature, love of variety	**Arc base** avoids responsibility, clannish	**Number 9** good with figures, musical, good taste
Short tail sublimated sex drive, low energy levels	**Figure 8** quick thinker with humor and a taste for culture	**Like a "q"** kind, caring, altruistic, some sexual repression
Large loop money-bags, emotional involvement	**No loop** if light, weak will; if heavy, determined, temper	**Hooked final** collector, egotistical, likes own way
Unusual loop compulsive, unusual sexual tastes	**Triangular** judgmental, difficult to live with or get along with	**X-loop** unhappy with physical appearance, poor sex life, depressive

The letter

A consistently made letter "h" with the upper stroke reasonably well-aligned with the general slant of the script is indicative of ambition and good self-control. Slight differences show the writer to pursue his or her ideas but if the construction of the letter varies widely the author will be inclined to follow impractical plans and schemes.

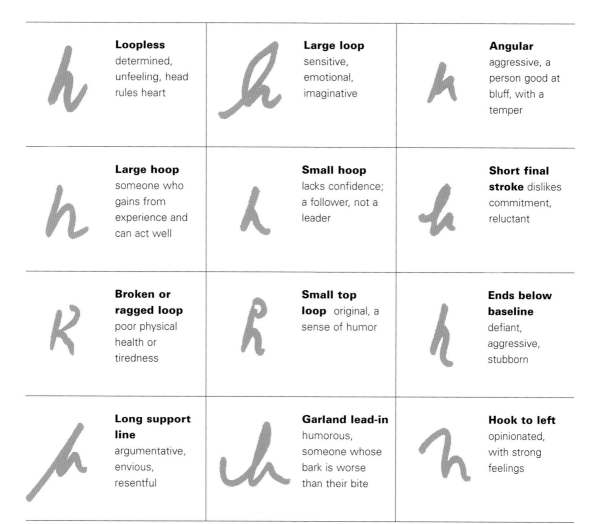

Loopless
determined, unfeeling, head rules heart

Large loop
sensitive, emotional, imaginative

Angular
aggressive, a person good at bluff, with a temper

Large hoop
someone who gains from experience and can act well

Small hoop
lacks confidence; a follower, not a leader

Short final stroke dislikes commitment, reluctant

Broken or ragged loop
poor physical health or tiredness

Small top loop original, a sense of humor

Ends below baseline
defiant, aggressive, stubborn

Long support line
argumentative, envious, resentful

Garland lead-in
humorous, someone whose bark is worse than their bite

Hook to left
opinionated, with strong feelings

The letter *i*

The size of the letter "i" is important. When consistently smaller than other middle zone letters, the writer will exhibit inner insecurity and worry. When written the same size or larger, expect to find confidence and inner poise. It is quite normal to see up to five or more variations in the way the letter is written.

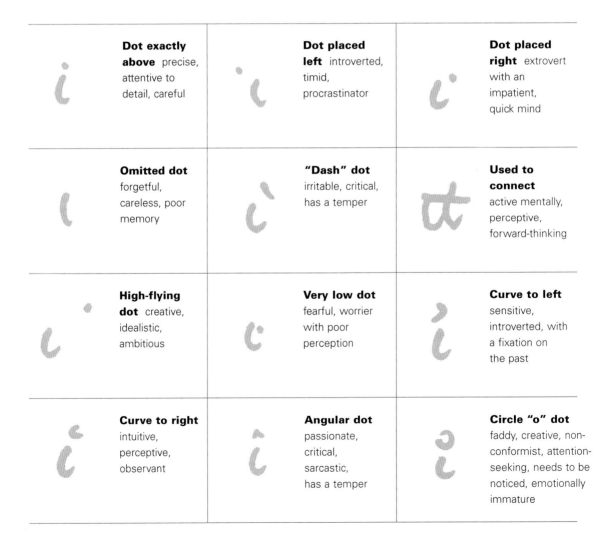

Dot exactly above precise, attentive to detail, careful

Dot placed left introverted, timid, procrastinator

Dot placed right extrovert with an impatient, quick mind

Omitted dot forgetful, careless, poor memory

"Dash" dot irritable, critical, has a temper

Used to connect active mentally, perceptive, forward-thinking

High-flying dot creative, idealistic, ambitious

Very low dot fearful, worrier with poor perception

Curve to left sensitive, introverted, with a fixation on the past

Curve to right intuitive, perceptive, observant

Angular dot passionate, critical, sarcastic, has a temper

Circle "o" dot faddy, creative, non-conformist, attention-seeking, needs to be noticed, emotionally immature

The letter *j*

The "j" should be read in much the same way as the letters "f," "g," and "y" when assessing the writer's physical energy, libido, and attention to everyday affairs. Dots, when used, should be read in the same way as the letter "i." The shape of the letter will give an insight into the level of the writer's inner emotional balance.

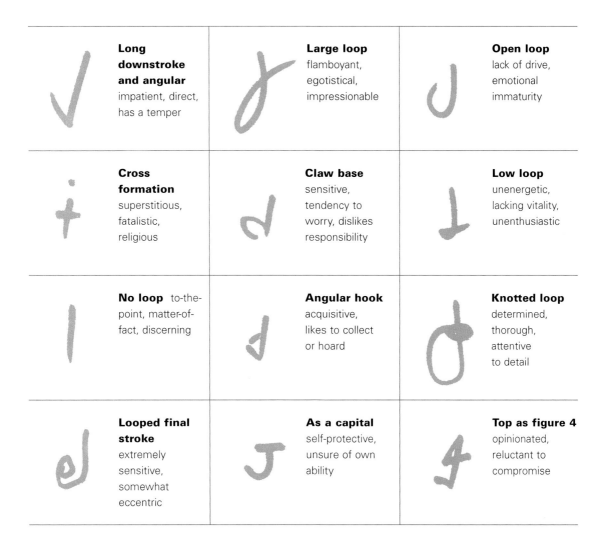

Long downstroke and angular
impatient, direct, has a temper

Large loop
flamboyant, egotistical, impressionable

Open loop
lack of drive, emotional immaturity

Cross formation
superstitious, fatalistic, religious

Claw base
sensitive, tendency to worry, dislikes responsibility

Low loop
unenergetic, lacking vitality, unenthusiastic

No loop to-the-point, matter-of-fact, discerning

Angular hook
acquisitive, likes to collect or hoard

Knotted loop
determined, thorough, attentive to detail

Looped final stroke
extremely sensitive, somewhat eccentric

As a capital
self-protective, unsure of own ability

Top as figure 4
opinionated, reluctant to compromise

The letter *k*

Variations in the way the letter "k" is written show poor physical and emotional control on the part of the writer, so the more consistently it is created, the more balanced the writer. This is a good letter to help the analyst determine the level of physical affection someone may have for others and how stubborn the person can be.

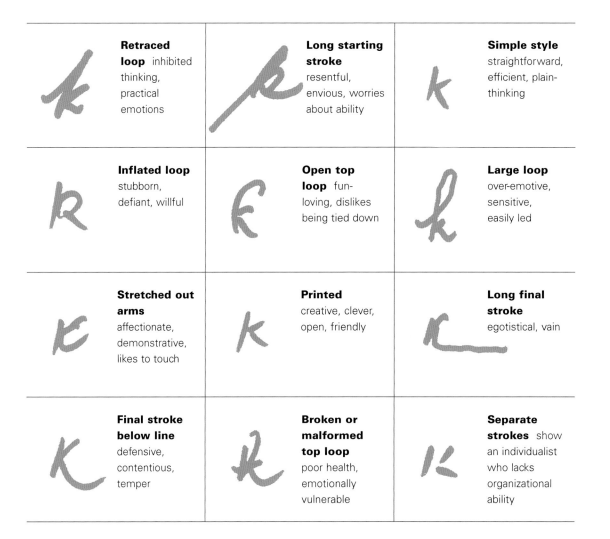

Retraced loop inhibited thinking, practical emotions	**Long starting stroke** resentful, envious, worries about ability	**Simple style** straightforward, efficient, plain-thinking
Inflated loop stubborn, defiant, willful	**Open top loop** fun-loving, dislikes being tied down	**Large loop** over-emotive, sensitive, easily led
Stretched out arms affectionate, demonstrative, likes to touch	**Printed** creative, clever, open, friendly	**Long final stroke** egotistical, vain
Final stroke below line defensive, contentious, temper	**Broken or malformed top loop** poor health, emotionally vulnerable	**Separate strokes** show an individualist who lacks organizational ability

The letter *l*

The lower case "l" is written with a loop, which always indicates emotion. When two letters written together are consistent, they indicate that their writer controls themselves well. But when they are not written consistently, their writer cannot control their feelings properly. This suggests there is an absence of certain convictions in the person.

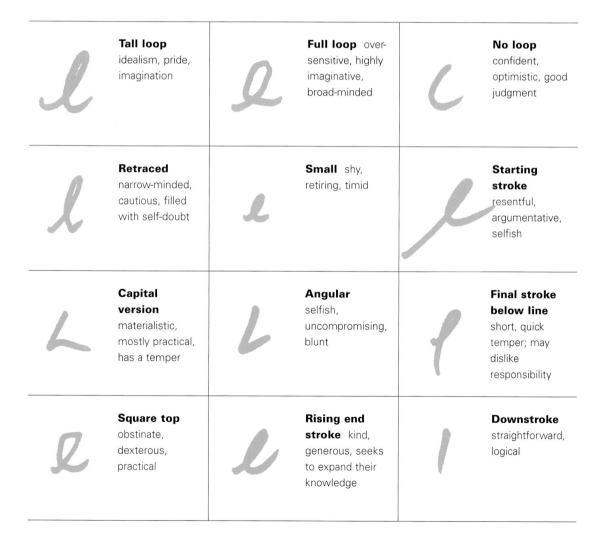

Tall loop
idealism, pride, imagination

Full loop over-sensitive, highly imaginative, broad-minded

No loop
confident, optimistic, good judgment

Retraced
narrow-minded, cautious, filled with self-doubt

Small shy, retiring, timid

Starting stroke
resentful, argumentative, selfish

Capital version
materialistic, mostly practical, has a temper

Angular
selfish, uncompromising, blunt

Final stroke below line
short, quick temper; may dislike responsibility

Square top
obstinate, dexterous, practical

Rising end stroke kind, generous, seeks to expand their knowledge

Downstroke
straightforward, logical

The letter *m*

The way this letter is created shows how the writer reacts to the opinions of others. A low first arch suggests dependency on what they think or say, while a low second arch indicates a more independent nature. A broad letter "m" means the writer is extravagant, while a narrow version indicates a more retiring or cautious nature. Two letters appearing together that are consistent show inner contentment.

No middle bar avoids responsibility, loves freedom

Angular leadership, impatience, poor humor

Three arches worry, insecurity, compulsiveness

Inwardly curved end stroke critical nature, fault-finder

First arch high pride, poor taste, worries what others think

Second arch high needs constant praise, self-conscious

Like a "v" or "w" health conscious, faddy, superficial

Musical note musical interest or ability

Middle loop controlling nature, worries about others

Short final stroke avoids responsibility and involvement

Modern style fond of culture, admires form and shape

Pointed arches inquisitive, perceptive, likes to learn

The letter *n*

This letter is often used to gauge the size of middle zone handwriting. A wide letter suggests expansiveness, while a narrow one implies caution. It often ends a sentence slightly larger than the words preceding it, indicating childishness and immaturity.

When the letter "n" is repeated within a word and does not appear consistent, it implies a lack of stability and a possible emotional imbalance in its writer, perhaps even childishness again.

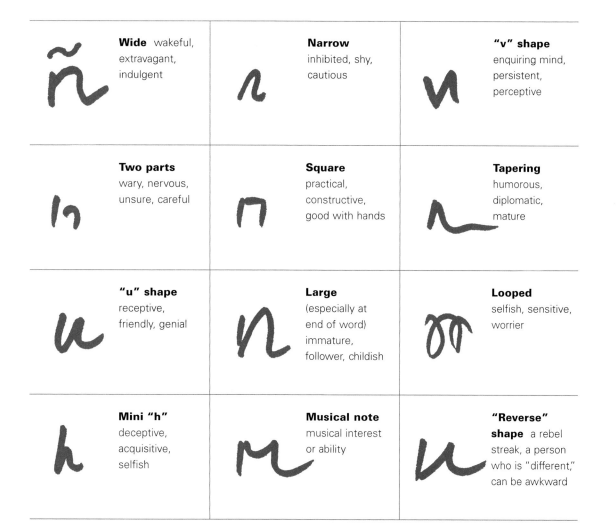

Wide wakeful, extravagant, indulgent	**Narrow** inhibited, shy, cautious	**"v" shape** enquiring mind, persistent, perceptive
Two parts wary, nervous, unsure, careful	**Square** practical, constructive, good with hands	**Tapering** humorous, diplomatic, mature
"u" shape receptive, friendly, genial	**Large** (especially at end of word) immature, follower, childish	**Looped** selfish, sensitive, worrier
Mini "h" deceptive, acquisitive, selfish	**Musical note** musical interest or ability	**"Reverse" shape** a rebel streak, a person who is "different," can be awkward

The letter o

The middle zone letter "o" reveals the amount of honesty and commitment a writer has. When two "o" letters are written together, but are obviously different, the writer places personal interests before those of others. If, during the course of what is written, double letters are connected in the same style, the writer is fairly honest and exhibits a certain amount of self-control.

Broken base someone dishonest, untrustworthy, cunning	**Two parts** hypocrisy, a person who takes advantages	**Full** tolerant, broad-minded, discreet
Open top sincere but talkative, gullible	**Open to right** blunt, to-the-point, direct	**Open to left** an indiscreet gossip, chatterbox
Crossed top acquisitive, bold, not always reliable	**Small or narrow** narrow-minded, tight-fisted, cautious	**Loops in oval** deceptive inner nature, sarcasm, poor discipline
Inside line perceptive, shrewd, can be evasive	**Pear shape** little enthusiasm, low boredom threshold	**Horseshoe** controlling, at the forefront, likes to be noticed

The letter *p*

The letter "p" will show how much appreciation the writer has for the physical, sports, or outdoor aspects of life. A poorly formed "p" often appears when someone is tired. When two letter "p"s are together, they usually have the same appearance. If not, their author is likely to be inconsistent or even unpredictable at times and may be uncoordinated.

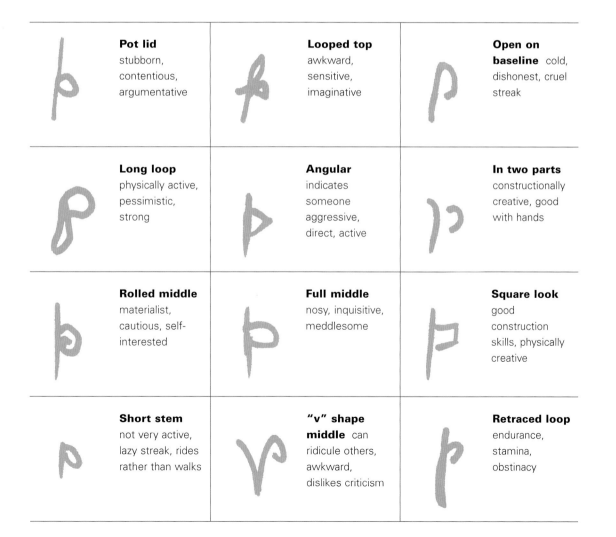

Pot lid stubborn, contentious, argumentative	**Looped top** awkward, sensitive, imaginative	**Open on baseline** cold, dishonest, cruel streak
Long loop physically active, pessimistic, strong	**Angular** indicates someone aggressive, direct, active	**In two parts** constructionally creative, good with hands
Rolled middle materialist, cautious, self-interested	**Full middle** nosy, inquisitive, meddlesome	**Square look** good construction skills, physically creative
Short stem not very active, lazy streak, rides rather than walks	**"v" shape middle** can ridicule others, awkward, dislikes criticism	**Retraced loop** endurance, stamina, obstinacy

The letter q

How writers write the letter "q" indicates the amount of sensitivity, self-confidence, and belief in their own ability that they have. The "q" is frequently poorly written. Whatever shape writers adopt, it is not always penned consistently. Variations are often a key to the lengths to which people will take a bluff.

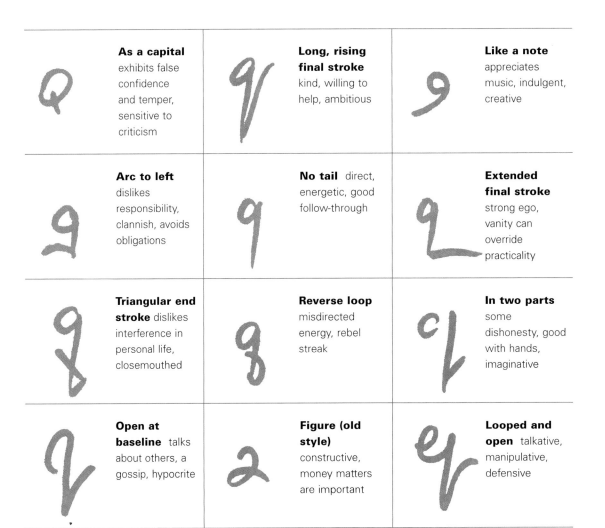

As a capital exhibits false confidence and temper, sensitive to criticism

Long, rising final stroke kind, willing to help, ambitious

Like a note appreciates music, indulgent, creative

Arc to left dislikes responsibility, clannish, avoids obligations

No tail direct, energetic, good follow-through

Extended final stroke strong ego, vanity can override practicality

Triangular end stroke dislikes interference in personal life, closemouthed

Reverse loop misdirected energy, rebel streak

In two parts some dishonesty, good with hands, imaginative

Open at baseline talks about others, a gossip, hypocrite

Figure (old style) constructive, money matters are important

Looped and open talkative, manipulative, defensive

The letter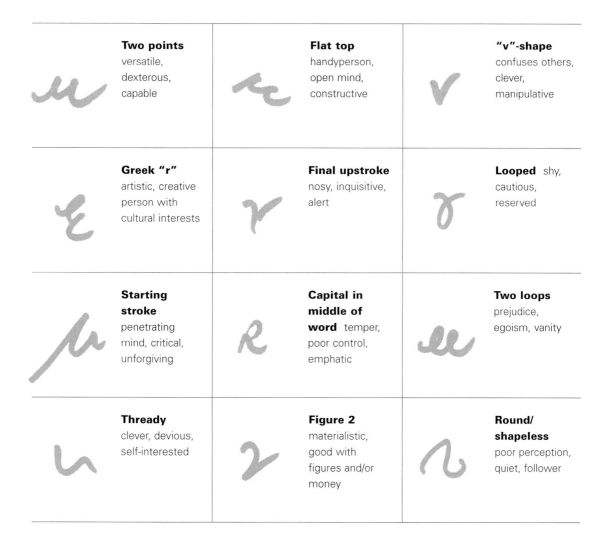

In normal handwriting, the letter "r" may take on four or five variations of shapes and styles. However, any more than that points to inconsistencies in the writer's self-control and ability to concentrate. Well-made letters point to good levels of self-control—someone not to be trifled with. There is often a fair degree of manual dexterity when the letter "r" is well-formed.

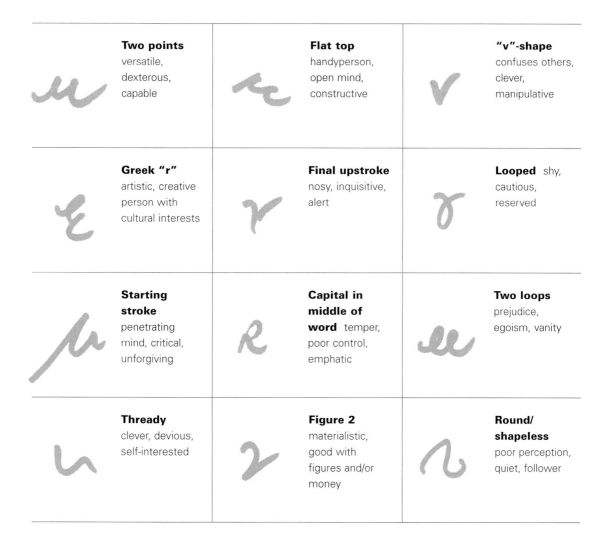

Two points versatile, dexterous, capable	**Flat top** handyperson, open mind, constructive	**"v"-shape** confuses others, clever, manipulative
Greek "r" artistic, creative person with cultural interests	**Final upstroke** nosy, inquisitive, alert	**Looped** shy, cautious, reserved
Starting stroke penetrating mind, critical, unforgiving	**Capital in middle of word** temper, poor control, emphatic	**Two loops** prejudice, egoism, vanity
Thready clever, devious, self-interested	**Figure 2** materialistic, good with figures and/or money	**Round/ shapeless** poor perception, quiet, follower

The letter s

The letter "s" should be executed in the same style throughout a writing sample, but slight variations are often seen and are quite acceptable. In order to indicate self-control and maturity, two letters appearing consecutively should be similarly constructed. When the last letter of a word is an "s," and is larger than others being used, it can imply childishness.

Open at baseline gullible, poor perception, easy-going	**Closed at baseline** careful, diligent, watchful	**Rounded** gentle, yielding, kind
Like a pawn sharp-tongued, sarcastic, prejudiced	**Hook at start** individualistic, resentful, has own rules	**Final loop upward** determined, set in ways, a "must-win" attitude
Angular aggressive, angry, perverse	**Closed** doesn't listen, secretive, selfish	**Figure 8** good with figures and money, materialistic
Simple tasteful, diplomatic, has cultural interests	**Dollar sign** collector, acquisitive, loves money	**Arc or claw at baseline** dislikes responsibility, avoids obligations

The letter *t*

There are well over 400 ways to create the letter "t". This most important contribution to handwriting analysis allows us to deduce ambition, control, drive, intelligence, speed, and will-power. It is rarely created in the same style, whether at the beginning, middle, or end of a word, so one must observe it very carefully indeed.

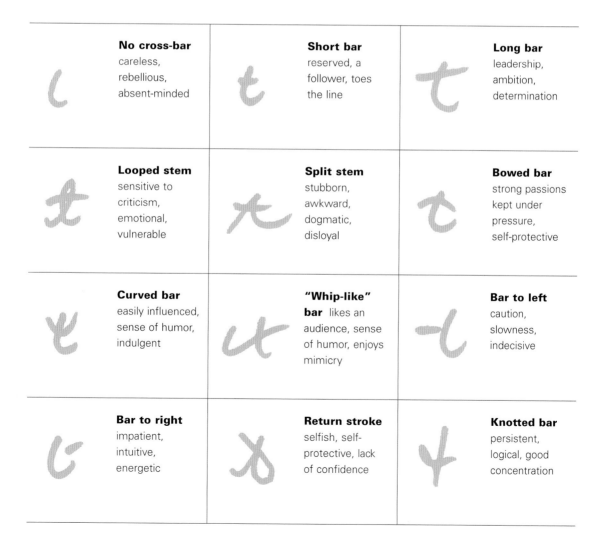

No cross-bar
careless, rebellious, absent-minded

Short bar
reserved, a follower, toes the line

Long bar
leadership, ambition, determination

Looped stem
sensitive to criticism, emotional, vulnerable

Split stem
stubborn, awkward, dogmatic, disloyal

Bowed bar
strong passions kept under pressure, self-protective

Curved bar
easily influenced, sense of humor, indulgent

"Whip-like" bar likes an audience, sense of humor, enjoys mimicry

Bar to left
caution, slowness, indecisive

Bar to right
impatient, intuitive, energetic

Return stroke
selfish, self-protective, lack of confidence

Knotted bar
persistent, logical, good concentration

The letter *u*

The letter "u" often appears slightly larger in the majority of average handwriting, which suggests some uncertainty in the writer's overall approach to everyday problems. When much smaller than an average middle zone letter, its writer will appear to be much more confident than most people. If joined to the preceding or succeeding letter, its author blends in well socially.

Garland socially orientated, friendly, open	**Angular** awkward, persistent, stubborn	**Small/narrow** shy, may dislike new experiences
Low and wide ready for anything fresh or new, Jack-of-all-trades	**Large and deep** imaginative, dramatic, full of ideas	**Square** good with hands, practical, down-to-earth
Looped manipulative, deceiving	**Starting stroke** aggressive, resentful, pettily envious	**Horseshoe** petty disciplinarian, conservative
Tall first stroke superficial confidence, vain	**Tall final stroke** enterprising, takes chances	**Inwardly curved end stroke** self-defensive, self-protective, uncertain

The letter 𝓊

Despite being an angular letter, the letter "v" is often created in a more rounded manner than is usually expected. This letter is very useful to help discern someone's level of emotional energy, for a strong and widely penned "v" is a good indication of a healthy sexual nature, both physically and emotionally, especially if not connected to other letters within the word.

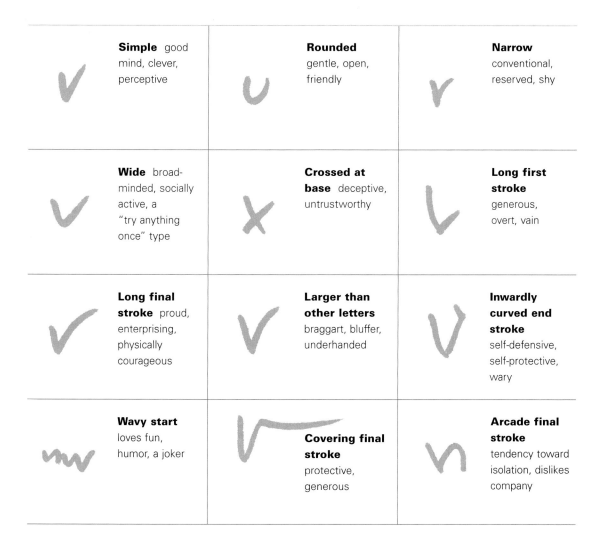

Simple good mind, clever, perceptive

Rounded gentle, open, friendly

Narrow conventional, reserved, shy

Wide broad-minded, socially active, a "try anything once" type

Crossed at base deceptive, untrustworthy

Long first stroke generous, overt, vain

Long final stroke proud, enterprising, physically courageous

Larger than other letters braggart, bluffer, underhanded

Inwardly curved end stroke self-defensive, self-protective, wary

Wavy start loves fun, humor, a joker

Covering final stroke protective, generous

Arcade final stroke tendency toward isolation, dislikes company

The letter *w*

The "w" helps a graphologist assess the level of enthusiasm, defensiveness, and compensatory powers that writers have. It shows whether they expect too much or are insecure, and whether they are leaders or easily led. The way this letter is created is a useful guide because, in young people especially, it can help you decide whether someone has tendencies toward having a bullying nature or being a bullied victim.

Curved end stroke self-protective, defensive nature	**Tall end stroke** enterprising, proud, courageous	**Tall first stroke** arrogant, vain, impetuous
Looped smooth, manipulative, a bluffer	**Inwardly curved** holds on to past too much, unable to let go	**Arches** self-protective, difficult to get to know, secretive
Starting stroke envious, needs to be convinced, aggressive	**Final loop** arty, theatrical, needs to be different to others	**Rounded** gentle, shy, friendly
Angular alert, shrewd, analytical	**Crossed middle** egotist, show-off, falsely modest	**Broad** extravagant, wasteful, too open-minded

The letter x

When the "x"-formation is found in any handwriting, it is a sure sign of depression, feelings of failure, and inadequacy or emotional vulnerability. A large, boldly written letter is usually a sign of good health, determination, and strength of character. A small or poorly penned "x" letter shows defeatism, although this may be due to just a temporary mood the writer is suffering.

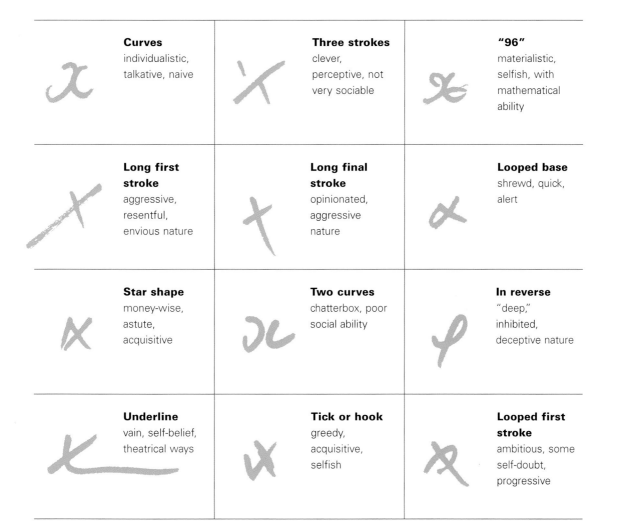

Curves
individualistic, talkative, naive

Three strokes
clever, perceptive, not very sociable

"96"
materialistic, selfish, with mathematical ability

Long first stroke
aggressive, resentful, envious nature

Long final stroke
opinionated, aggressive nature

Looped base
shrewd, quick, alert

Star shape
money-wise, astute, acquisitive

Two curves
chatterbox, poor social ability

In reverse
"deep," inhibited, deceptive nature

Underline
vain, self-belief, theatrical ways

Tick or hook
greedy, acquisitive, selfish

Looped first stroke
ambitious, some self-doubt, progressive

The letter *y*

The sexual nature of the writer is assessed within the letter "y", for it can indicate repression, tension, or imagination, and even aberration, according to the way it is created. Many graphologists also use this letter to discern a writer's degree of introversion or extroversion, responsibility or irresponsibility, through assessing its overall form and appearance.

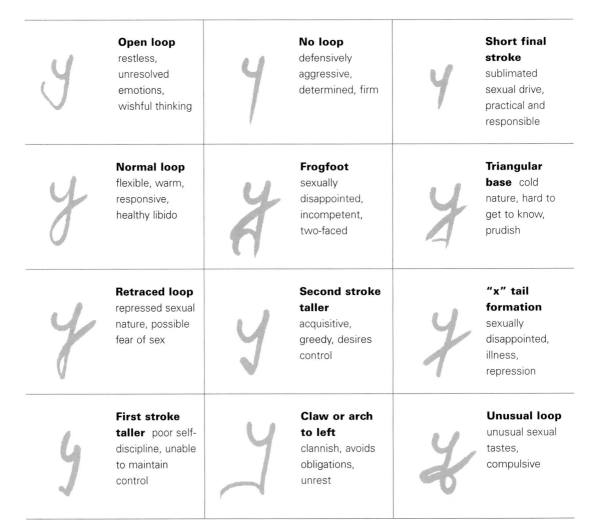

Open loop
restless, unresolved emotions, wishful thinking

No loop
defensively aggressive, determined, firm

Short final stroke
sublimated sexual drive, practical and responsible

Normal loop
flexible, warm, responsive, healthy libido

Frogfoot
sexually disappointed, incompetent, two-faced

Triangular base cold nature, hard to get to know, prudish

Retraced loop
repressed sexual nature, possible fear of sex

Second stroke taller
acquisitive, greedy, desires control

"x" tail formation
sexually disappointed, illness, repression

First stroke taller poor self-discipline, unable to maintain control

Claw or arch to left
clannish, avoids obligations, unrest

Unusual loop
unusual sexual tastes, compulsive

The letter z

Read the letter "z" to assess its writers' resistance to emotional and mental pressure. Although rarely seen twice in the same sample, when it is written in the same manner consistently, it indicates consistency of approach, sound judgment, and that the writer's opinions are worth listening to. When poorly made, it suggests a reluctance to criticize or give advice.

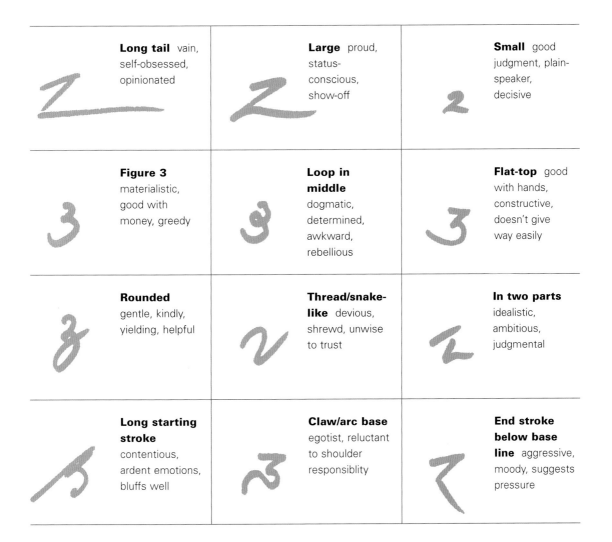

Long tail vain, self-obsessed, opinionated

Large proud, status-conscious, show-off

Small good judgment, plain-speaker, decisive

Figure 3 materialistic, good with money, greedy

Loop in middle dogmatic, determined, awkward, rebellious

Flat-top good with hands, constructive, doesn't give way easily

Rounded gentle, kindly, yielding, helpful

Thread/snake-like devious, shrewd, unwise to trust

In two parts idealistic, ambitious, judgmental

Long starting stroke contentious, ardent emotions, bluffs well

Claw/arc base egotist, reluctant to shoulder responsiblity

End stroke below base line aggressive, moody, suggests pressure

Numbers

Numbers and the way they are written are indicative of how writers express their orientation to material assets and values. The degree of talent they have in the sciences and the arts may also be discerned here.

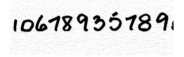

Clearly drawn numbers When numbers are written clearly and without embellishment, they suggest a reliable and honest character. A person who writes numbers this way is usually well qualified to deal with material and monetary matters, and will do so carefully.

Badly drawn numbers Conversely, someone who draws numbers badly will have difficulty handling a budget properly and therefore should not be trusted with other people's assets. This does not mean that the writer is dishonest. Far from it, the person is simply likely to be indifferent to numbers, or else unable to comprehend the intricacies of money matters.

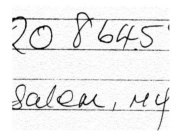

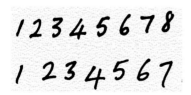

Large numbers Large numbers written with heavy pressure indicate materialistic types, people who know the price and value of almost everything they touch. Such writers do not fully understand money and its proper use and will be inclined to be far too generous for their own good.

Small numbers Small numbers, especially if smaller than the main body of script and etched lightly on paper, reveal the ability to concentrate and focus on monetary matters. Writers who do this may be very careful with their finances and personal property, for this is often the style of accountants or people who deal with mathematics.

Arrangement on baseline Like ordinary handwriting, numbers should be written across a page on an even baseline. People who do this get things done quickly and are able to plan ahead logically. Uneven baselines reflect poor control. If the baseline slants upward, the writer is a born optimist, while one that slants downward is usually a sign of pessimism.

12345678

Square appearance Whether written large or small, a square look to numbers indicates technical or mechanical appreciation and ability.

3	5	4
7	3	6
8	6	7
1	8	7
6	9	7
4	4	6
3	3	3
		4

Numbers in columns Columns of numbers should be written carefully, one under the other all the way down the page with the same slant as the script. When a column begins to move back to the left of the page, it shows a concern with security. People who write columns this way like to hold on to their possessions. If columns veer toward the right of the page, their writers want to move on with things and progress at their own pace; they can be impatient and make mistakes.

Faint numbers Indistinct or touched-up numbers indicate a worrying and careless mentality. Once again, this does not mean a dishonest character, only someone who should not be allowed to work with money, theirs or that of others, because mistakes are much more likely to be made. If writers do not always make such embellishments, they have resolved the problems that were worrying them at the time they wrote them.

24th March 196
15th May 1971
27th September 1

The interpretation of numbers

1 / 1 / 1 1

Number *1*

Many authorities like to compare the number one with the personal pronoun "I" (or PPI). Normally made as a single stroke, its slant should fit in with the rest of the script. Sometimes it is made from the bottom upward—always a sign of a rebel streak. People who put a small support line underneath the number one tend to work carefully and like to stick to the rules. A figure that ends below the baseline shows poor control, or else a writer who may have been tired at the time of writing it. A hook on any part of the number is a sign of irritability and temper. A dot at the top shows a momentary hesitation that could indicate self-doubt, or someone who likes to check things first before starting any task.

2 2 2 2 2

Number *2*

Small loops at the top indicate a degree of envy. The larger the loop, the more this will be evident. A flat, straight base shows stability, while an arch at the bottom suggests resourcefulness. If the arch is made with a loop at the bottom, the writer will be protective. A large loop here always signals this. A long baseline extending to the right implies an over-generous nature. If the tail of the number dips below the baseline, the writer may lack a sense of responsibility or avoid it altogether.

Number 3

If the half-loop at the top is bigger than the bottom, it shows imagination, someone full of ideas. When the lower part is larger, the writer is more concerned with daily life. If a little loop ties the two big loops together, the writer may be impractical. Mechanical skills may be present when the top line is flat rather than curved. A long extension as an end stroke to the left of the figure shows a concern with past issues.

Number 4

This number is associated with everyday life and can reveal a love of discussion. An angular number shows an aggressive mentality. A "triangle on a leg" indicates intellect, imagination, and originality. A poorly written number implies inner confusion. Curves anywhere in this number denote a sense of being "different," and are somewhat akin to the circle "i"-dot.

Number 5

Some people write this number without lifting pen from paper, while others draw the bulk of it first and add a top like the freestyle cross of the letter "t." A short top bar indicates a temper, while a long one implies aggression. A hook at the start shows irritability, a curved bar means humor. If the bowl of the number strays into the lower zone, it indicates a sensualist.

Number 6

This number is created very much like the letter "b." When the loop is closed by the tail passing through the back stroke, there will be a touch of possessiveness, possibly brought about by jealousy. The main bowl of the number should occupy the middle zone, while the extender pushes into the upper zone; the higher it stretches, the more ambitious the writer's nature. An open bowl shows procrastination, while a small one implies inner tensions.

Number 7

A seven may be made in one movement, where the writer starts at the top left-hand side, moves over to the right, and either makes a small loop or just comes straight down to the baseline—or beyond it. Sometimes the top bar looks slightly wavy like a capital letter "T", which suggests a responsible nature. If it is a large loop, this may be tinged with envy. A loop at the joint of the top bar and the down stroke implies a lack of staying power. If the down stroke ends below the baseline, the writer will show an ability with figures. In the UK, a cross bar on the down stroke is a sign of affectation.

Number 8

This number should be drawn with two well-balanced circles, one above the other, reflecting a generally balanced outlook. When the bottom circle is larger, the emphasis is on physical or day-to-day interests, but if the upper loop is dominant, the nature is more idealistic and imaginative. If the upper circle is open at the top, the writer is talkative but open-minded. When open to the left, there will be some introversion, while if open to the right, it implies extroversion.

Number 9

This is written in a similar manner to the lower case letter "g," but can end in a straight down stroke made like a reversed number 6 that occasionally strays into the lower zone. A rounded number shows a talkative nature, while an angular version implies a temper. A short tail suggests little effort and poor follow-through. A long tail to the left marks concern with past events and the people involved.

Number 0

The number zero is very much like the lower case letter "o," and the reader is recommended to read one as such. In addition, two zeros that are tied together by a bar or a knot suggests monetary and mathematical ability. If any part of the zero looks too straight, the writer may be undergoing some emotional problems.

Like signatures, all examples of numbers must be read in conjunction with the rest of the script, for numbers written by themselves can be misleading.

Glossary

Air stroke Where the line of writing disappears because of lack of pressure.

Angular script Handwriting with sharp lines and few curves.

Arcade script Curved handwriting with the appearance of a row of arches like a long line of the letter "m."

Ascender A stroke, line, or loop that reaches into the upper zone.

Baseline The imaginary horizontal line from the left-hand side of the page to the right created by a writer.

Block capital An upper case letter that has been printed rather than written in the cursive style.

Body of script The main block of text in any written missive.

Broad script Wide handwriting.

Concave script A line of handwriting that begins at the baseline, eases below, and then rises again.

Connectedness A line of handwriting where the majority of letters or words are connected, usually by a stroke.

Convex script A line of handwriting that rises from the baseline, then sinks again.

Copybook The basic style of handwriting, varying from country to country and also from region to region.

Cover stroke Ascending or descending stroke written over by the return stroke; often narrows an intended loop.

Curlicue An additional decoration to a letter formation.

Descender A stroke, line, or loop that reaches into the lower zone.

Diacritic A mark (like an accent or cedilla) to indicate a different sound of a letter.

Disconnected script A line of writing where the majority of letters are not joined together.

Ductus A graphological term for the line of ink in handwriting.

Embellishment An additional decoration to a letter formation.

Form level The overall standard of appearance of a sample of handwritten text.

Garland script A rounded handwriting style with the appearance of a row of upside-down arches—like a series of the letter "w."

Greek form A type of letter formation in the Greek style—usually the letters "d," "e," and "g."

Hook A starting or finishing mark like a forward or backward check mark.

Horizontal zone Where the width of handwriting is observed (can be broad, medium, or narrow).

Layout The way a letter or other handwriting sample is set out on a page.

Loops Curved strokes or loops that may appear in all three zones and that always indicate some emotion.

Lower zone Area below the baseline where descenders from the letters "g," "j," "p," "q," "y," and "z" are seen.

Middle zone Area immediately above the baseline usually occupied by the middle part of a letter. The letters "a," "c," "e," "m," "n," "o," "r," "s," "u," "v," "w," and "x" occupy this zone in their entirety.

Mingling Occurs when upper zone ascenders mix in with the lower zone descenders from the line above.

Narrow script Handwriting compressed along the baseline.

Neglected script Simplified handwriting that, while legible, may often omit necessary or accepted strokes.

Ovals Letters or parts of letters that are round in shape.

Paraph A mark made after a signature—usually an underline.

Pasty Thick writing like that made with a fiber tip marker, pencil, or fountain pen with a wide nib.

Post-placed "i"-dots or "t"-bars made to the right of the stem of the letter.

Potlid A letter with an extra long upper or lower stem creating the impression of a pot with a wide lid lying on its side.

PPI The personal pronoun "I."

Pre-placed "i"-dots or "t"-bars made to the left of the stem of the letter.

Pressure The weight with which a pen stroke has been applied to the page.

Punctuation Recognized grammatical marks used in handwriting.

Regularity Uniformity of appearance in handwriting.

Resting point A small mark made by a pen when allowed to pause during normal handwriting.

Rhythmic script Handwriting with a distinctively fluid, harmonious appearance.

Roofing A flourish or extended mark over the top of a letter, word or series of words, for example, the top bar of the capital letter "T."

Script Handwriting as opposed to print.

Signature The regular way a person writes his or her name, or personal mark.

Size ratio The relative proportions of handwriting; the accepted norm is 3 mm per zone thus creating a total possible average letter size of 9 mm.

Slant Describes the angle at which handwriting inclines or reclines.

Spacing The distance between letters, lines, or words.

Stem The upright section of a letter as seen in the "d," "i," or "t."

Stepped script Handwriting where each letter or word appears at a slightly different level along the baseline, either upward or downward.

Stroke The line made by the pen (broken or unbroken), or small extra mark employed by a writer to create some or all letters.

Thread script Handwriting that deteriorates into illegibility in the middle or at the end of a word.

Triangle The angular formation of an upper or lower loop.

Upper zone The area above the middle zone where the ascending strokes of the letters "b," "d," "f," "h," "k," "l," and "t" are made.

Vertical script Handwriting that does not incline or recline more than five degrees from the upright.

Zones The divisions in a line of handwriting used by a graphologist to determine different characteristics of individual letters (see lower, middle, and upper zones).

Chatty, excitable, envious hardworking, imaginative, selfish, trustworthy, obstinate, unreliable, jealous, greedy, ... , upbeat, excitable

Index

a

b

c

d

e

f

g

h

i

j

l

m

Disclaimer

It would be impossible to find all, if any, of those people who have had examples of their handwriting or signatures used for material within these pages.

Where the author has made references to emphasize certain graphological points, it has been with that intention only in mind. No personal criticism of an individual has been intended.

The author and the publishers accept no liability for the accuracy or safety of any of the information or advice contained in, or in any way relating to any part of the content, of this book.